CHRISTIAN
ABC's

**Foundational Truths Every
Christian Should Know**

Andre Valentine Sr.

CHRISTIAN ABC'S

Copyright © 2013 **Andre Valentine Sr.**

Library of Congress Number: 2013939084

ISBN: 978-0-9890300-0-7

First Edition 2013.

All Scriptures Quoted from NASB

deepertruths.org

Mailing address:

Deeper Truths Publishing
P.O. Box 6611
Kent WA 98031

DEDICATION

To my mom, thank you for your inspiration. You taught me how to study the Bible using a Concordance and a Lexicon. These tools have become invaluable to me in my studies.

To my wife Valeria, thank you for your love, support, encouragement and strength. You were there for me in my darkest hour. It is because of you that I began to express myself through written form again.

I love you both with all my heart.

CONTENTS

Preface

Years ago, my mother moved my brothers and me from Milwaukee, Wisconsin to Little Rock, Arkansas in pursuit of greater spiritual knowledge. It was at the Word of Outreach Center that profound men of God would spend years instructing me.

My initial baptism into truths that I had never heard began with a teaching on six principles that would forever change the way I viewed the basic principles of doctrine in the Bible.

As I spent years learning and communicating this doctrine, I began to see the need for believers throughout the world to understand these principles, mentioned in the epistle to the Hebrews. I began to learn in order to teach. Suddenly, with crystal clarity, I saw my responsibility to the Body as recorded in the epistle to the Ephesians (Eph. 4:11-13).

According to the Holy Scriptures in Ephesians 4:11-13, God has given men and women as gifts to the body of Christ for the specific purpose of communicating instructions to the saints in order for them to become preoccupied with promoting the cause of Christ. Being in the office of a Teacher, I desire to carry out this God given mandate, realizing that the need for teaching saints by qualified teachers is immense. Such need will continue until our Lord returns from Heaven.

In this study, we are going to examine the basics concerning the doctrine of Christ as presented in the epistle to the Hebrews. If you desire to have our life, ministry and knowledge of the Word grounded effectively, you must be able to understand and appropriate these truths. Consequently, the principles that we will discuss directly affects the success of your life and ministry. Not success as people would define it, but success from God's perspective. Proper understanding of these ABC's of Christ will protect any church from many erroneous teachings; thus, ensuring that the leaders in the local assemblies will have an opportunity for success in their ministry.

There are primarily two things, which determine the success of any ministry: the quality of instruction given to the members and its ability to meet the needs of families. This book gives insight into the principle doctrines concerning Christ, which must form the core of all ministry and people building.

I have examined attentively the responses of believers who have received thorough instruction. Their eyes sparkle with excitement as they engage the "work of service". According to the Holy Scripture, preparing saints for this work is the goal the instructor has to keep in perspective. The "work of service" culminates in believers becoming spiritually mature.

However, this instruction must begin on a foundational platform; therefore, the author to the Hebrews reminds his hearers of the principles containing the most basic knowledge about Christ and his work.

Many believers desire to work for the Lord without first understanding the ABC's of the doctrine of Christ. This will have a severe negative affect on the establishment of any ministry. Without knowledge of these principles, we will be subject to gross error, substantially subjecting our beliefs to compromise, which must not be so.

I have dubbed these principles the ABC's because that is how they are defined in the book of Hebrews. These are the most basic teachings about Christ. Before you and I went on to any type of higher learning in school, one of the first things we learned was the ABCs. Why was this so important? The ABCs are the basic building blocks for all future learning. Consequently, if we did not understand letters of the alphabet, we could not learn to read. If we did not learn the basics of the English language, we would struggle with all future learning. This is what the author of the epistle to the Hebrews is attempting to get across to his readers. Doctrine concerning Christ does not get any more basic than these areas of instruction.

What you will observe is that these principles must become the foundation of all instruction for any believer who desires to mature completely in their understanding concerning Christ. In this book, we will examine the six principles located in the epistle to the Hebrews that begin the process of our spiritual development.

Although there are many different elementary principles presented in the Scriptures, these stand apart from the others. Teaching on such things as fasting, prayer and holiness are for living the proper Church life whereas the six principles in Hebrews are for knowledge and doctrine. Both types of principles help prepare us for the "work of service", but I have chosen to focus on the aspect of doctrine in this book. What you believe about Christ and his work will affect how you live.

While my years of studying these principles have brought changes to some of the ideas and concepts presented to me, many of the truths have remained the same. I am convinced that teaching these principles will properly prepare you for work in the ministry. This is my definitive desire.

The Christian ABC's is my simplistic attempt to communicate vital truths that have eternally affected my life. This book will radically change your life. It is my prayer that God may grant us the permit to build because we have shown due diligence in proper spiritual growth.

Serving the King,
Pastor Andre O. Valentine Sr.

ACKNOWLEDGMENTS

I am indebted to several people who, in various ways, contributed to the ideas in this book. My mentors, Robert E. Smith Sr., Pastor David Franklin and Elder William Caldwell have been influential in helping me understand these principles. Thank you. To my closest friend Maurice Pierce, you are an inspiration to me. Thank you for working with me through teaching these concepts and adding your insights into the development of this book.

TIME FOR SPIRITUAL MATURITY

Have you learned the basics concerning Christ to such an extent that you can comprehensively communicate them to others, ensuring that your brothers and sisters in Christ have the opportunity to grow from the same spiritual knowledge? If your answer is no then you need to continue reading this book because I wrote it especially for you.

Today we live in a world that is information driven. People are desperately searching for knowledge. We have moved from 3g to 4g. We have seen the 2nd generation of the iPad reach our hands in an attempt to get information to us quicker. Christian books of all types cram library shelves. Seminaries and universities are full of students desiring knowledge from the most educated professors. Our churches are full of preachers who have written books on eschatology, angelology, theology, Christology and how to turn your life around to experience prosperity. We can turn on the television and watch televangelists and pastors give sermons of every kind. There is an abundance of information.

Yet, a fundamental problem remains. With all this wealth of knowledge, many believers still fail to arrive at spiritual maturity. This is not a recent issue. This problem persisted with the disciples of Jesus Christ, the converts of Paul and such was the case in the book of Hebrews.

The author of the book of Hebrews challenges his audience to spiritual growth by writing the following words:

"For though by this time you ought to be teachers, you need again for someone to teach you the elementary principles of the oracles of God, and you have come to need milk and not solid food. For everyone who takes only of milk is not accustomed to the word of righteousness, for he is an infant. But solid food is for the mature, who because of practice have their senses trained to discern good and evil. Therefore leaving the elementary teaching about the Christ, let us press on to maturity, not laying again a foundation of repentance from dead works and of faith towards God, of instruction about washings and laying on of hands, and the resurrection of the dead and eternal judgement. And this we will do, if God permits" (Heb. 5:12-6:3).

You can tell if you are maturing spiritually by your ability to instruct others concerning what you have learned. Do you remember when you took a test in school? When your teacher put a question on the test that you had to answer in essay form, they wanted to see if you could properly communicate back to them the instruction they gave to you on let's say interpersonal communications in the work place. If you cannot write unambiguously about what you have learned on your test, then you did not grasp the information as the instructor intended. This is what the writer to the Hebrews attempted to get across to his hearers.

As you look at the foundational text, the writer wants to talk about deep things such as the comparison of Melchisedek, priest of Salem to Jesus. However, he understands that his audience is not capable of understanding this depth of information yet. He digresses from his discourse about Melchisedek and tells them, in essence, "You should have grown up by now." They had not. One of the greatest challenges for believers is to become spiritually mature.

While trying to maintain the work of grace in their hearts, they at times struggled with turning back to the rituals of the Law. Consequently, the writer gave this particular admonition to inspire these believers to continue moving forward in Christianity instead of looking back to Judaism like 1-year-old children who are afraid to leave their parents' side. Although they received instruction concerning the doctrine of Christ, like toddlers, many of them desired to remain close to the instructions that had been parenting them for their entire lives. In familiarity lies security. They did not want to leave the familiar for the foreign because of the uncertainty of how this new doctrine would work for them.

The underlying emphasis in the book of Hebrews is to let go of the past and live in the present. The author was exhorting them to recognize the changes that Christianity brought into their lives and to move forward in the spiritual comprehension of these truths. Sufficient time had elapsed. They should have grown by applying these truths and should be teaching other converts these same principles. This is the exhortation in Hebrews chapter ten. *"And let us consider how to stimulate one another to love and to good deeds ,not forsaking our own assembling together, as is the habit of some, but encouraging one another; and all the more as you see the day drawing near"*(Heb. 10:24, 25). However, this was not the case. They were not growing and teaching others, to the contrary, they needed to be educated again. This was a serious problem for the writer of this book and such is the case for many in the body of Christ today.

Some of you reading this book will struggle to leave

behind the religious instruction that has parented you for so long. However, only the maturing believer gains new perspectives based upon thorough investigation of new spiritual truths. As a maturing child of God, now is the time for you to grow in what you know and share these vital truths with others just as the writer of the book of Hebrews was propositioning his audience to do. The challenge for us today, as was to the Hebraic believers, is to grow up spiritually.

Again, the author comes to a pivotal juncture is his comparative analysis of Jesus' priesthood to the person of Melchisedek. He inserts a pause in his teaching session realizing that the spiritual condition and maturity of those he is writing to forbids him to transfer knowledge of such deep things (Heb. 5:11). I would imagine that he finds himself here at a place of utter frustration, having a wealth of knowledge that he wanted to communicate but unable to do so.

As a teacher (both of 5th grade boys and as a professor at a seminary), I have found that it can be an extremely frustrating scenario to be ready to teach knowledge; however, upon speaking, find that my students were unprepared to receive the information concerning the subject on which I desired to share.

My students and I understood that during each new day there must be some rehearsal of information previously conveyed. However, when I believed that my students should have grasped the information and there was much more review required than I expected, frustration sometimes overwhelmed me and I am sure some of my students as well.

It was very difficult to teach new material when many

my students did not understand information I had presented earlier. My students' ability to understand new material was hindered because they lacked comprehension about prior principles given. This is exactly what was happening in the book of Hebrews.

The exchanging of ideas that the author intended would result in a lengthy discourse and required an adequate ability to reason spiritually based upon the comprehension and application of prior truths. Realizing this, he begins to write concerning spiritual growth.

He deeply wanted his students to move on from their existing religious experiences through past ceremonies to a deeper spiritual experience via their union with Christ. No longer were they to live according to their rites under the old covenant. They were to live according to the education they received concerning the first principles of Christ.

The author wanted to feed them as much as he thought they could digest. Herein lays a problem within much of the Church today. Some leaders want to teach deep truths, but their hearers are unable to understand. Why did the believers in Hebrews not understand deeper truths? After years of instruction, they have failed to apply what they were taught about the doctrine of Christ; instead, they became people who needed to have those fundamental truths rehearsed to them again. Therefore, there is the need for the teaching concerning the founding elements of the doctrine concerning Christ.

The emphasis in this passage is not on one who is a slow learner even though they are applying themselves. What we see here is a student accustomed to one level of understanding who resists being elevated to the next level. They will not, and do not, apply themselves to understanding deeper and more fulfillling truths of the Scriptures.

The author says that his students were "dull of hearing" (5:11). This is a serious dilemma. On one hand, the things that the author wanted to communicate were "hard to explain". On the other hand, the hearers were "dull of hearing". Teaching had now become problematic. The comprehension level of the audience made it difficult for the writer to interpret Christ's priesthood to them. It was an exceedingly arduous task, and perhaps a daunting one.

"Dull of hearing" means to be sluggish or more literally "lazy". It refers to the difficulty of learning. Their problem was not an intellectual setback. These believers were simply lazy. This was the root cause of their difficulties in spiritual perception and understanding. They would not, and did not, take the truths taught and apply them, ensuring that they understood them and could receive greater revelatory truths.

Complex teaching to those who are of simple understanding will always pose a dilemma. People will either come up to a new level of understanding or become antagonistic towards the preacher and their preaching. To some extent, the people in the pews today have held preachers hostage. We have been limited in what we can teach, knowing that our audience is not capable of understanding certain truths. This problem is not something new.

God told the prophet Isaiah to speak these identical words to Israel. *"Go, and tell this people: 'Keep on listening, but do not perceive; Keep on looking, but do not understand'"* (Isa. 6:9). Israel repeatedly heard the words of God spoken through the mouth of Moses and other men of God. Yet, they did not apply themselves to understand His laws and commandments. As a result, hundreds of years later, because of the wickedness of their hearts, Isaiah gives them a prediction of their impending doom, showing us that people who are dull of hearing will suffer greatly. When preachers communicate truth, we have a responsibility to apply it. If we fail to employ them in our lives, we will not have sufficient spiritual comprehension to handle deeper truths. Without application, there is limited progression.

If you attend church on a weekly basis, listening to men and women of God who are instructing you about righteousness in the kingdom of God, and you continue to live a life of sin, which obviously contradicts the standard of righteousness, you are a modern day example of someone who is dull of hearing. This means that you refuse to know and experience this truth. Such a hard heart and closed mind make it difficult to understand more profound truths.

Jesus also ran into this identical problem when he was dialoguing with his disciples on one occasion. He said, *"I have many more things to say to you, but you cannot **bear** them now."*(John 16:12).The things that Jesus and the writer to the Hebrews desired to relate to their audience were not appropriate language for those they were attempting to teach. Both of their audiences did not have the ability to receive what which they were communicating.

If you look at the definition of the word "bear", a portion of the definition pertains to a person who is able to handle new truth cool, calm and collectively. Have you ever noticed how some people respond when someone tells them something they could not understand? At times, people will become irate or even indignant, showing their lack of calmness.

There may be individuals in the local church you attend

who constantly debate with you about scriptures. They not only fail to grow themselves but also attempt to contradict truth that the pastor gives because they themselves are not able to comprehend it. It appears as if they were saying, "If I cannot comprehend it, it must be wrong." This is the exact same thing the Pharisees and Sadducees did with Jesus. They argued with him, and even made attempts on his life, merely because they could not handle the depth of his teachings.

This is exactly what Jesus was attempting to avoid. It was the Lord's intention to give his hearers some equality with him in a certain level of his understanding; however, their spiritual capacity was insufficient to accommodate this depth of truth.

The most beloved apostle Paul found himself in a parallel scenario as the writer to the Hebrews and our Lord Jesus. He states to the believers at Corinth, *"I gave you milk to drink, not solid food; for you were not yet able to receive it. Indeed, even now you are not yet able..."* (1 Cor. 3:2). Paul addresses the same issue that Jesus faced. He tells the believers at Corinth that they could not handle the level of teaching Paul desired to transmit.

When Paul imparted the Christian faith, he had to do so with God-given skill and discretion. He did not merely write what he wanted to communicate. The apostle had to make responsible decisions concerning whether or not it was the right timing to give discourse on a particular subject. If he did not proceed with cautious reservations, his teachings could have had devastating results.

The truth we share as teachers of the faith needs to coincide with the level of knowledge the hearers possess. A university professor will not teach English 101 to students in the 5ᵗʰ grade. Those students need teaching about nouns, verbs and prepositions. Likewise, we should not speak about things that are too difficult for our audience to understand. Spiritually mature believers are the only ones who can understand a mature word.

Peter gives some words of insight concerning Paul's apostolic letters. He writes, "...*just as also our beloved brother Paul, according to the wisdom given him, hath wrote to you, as also in all his letters, speaking in them of these things, in which are some things hard to understand, which the untaught and unstable distort, as they do also the rest of the Scriptures, to their own destruction*" (2 Pet. 3:15, 16).

The apostle uses the words "hard to understand", whereas in our foundational text we see the words "hard to explain" (Heb. 5:11). In one sense, it is difficult for the teacher/preacher to explain deeper truths, while in another there is difficulty for the hearer to comprehend them. The struggle in explaining is not because the preachers do not know what they want to talk about, but because the perception of the hearers limits their communication.

Peter says this person has a deficiency in their ability to understand particular truths. People who are "untaught" and "unstable" do not possess sufficient knowledge to understand certain portions of scripture; consequently, they cannot grasp the deep revelation of God.

Due to the difficulty in comprehension, this person also begins to manipulate and degrade the Scripture into a false meaning. However the sincerity of one in attempting to understand particular truths of the Scriptures, to wrestle with a text is extremely unjust and dangerous. If believers attempt to digest certain truths without having a stable relationship with the Lord and a sufficient foundation, they will begin to twist and pervert truth.

These individuals ignorantly develop doctrinal error; refusing to correct it and will stand against all who attempt to address their theological issues. Therefore, as you shall see shortly, it becomes extremely important for you to grow in spiritual life and understanding if you are going to have a fuller comprehension of God's word.

I remember many years ago talking with a young man who was a recent recipient of salvation. He was extremely zealous for the things of God. However, he began to read some things in the book of Revelation and wanted to argue with me about them. He begins to talk to me about the first fruits of Revelation chapter 14. As he read that chapter, my friend came across the statement, *"These are the ones who have not been defiled with women, for they have kept themselves chaste"* (14:4). Immediately, he tells me that the only way you could attain to this special group was to be a virgin – literally. This was a problem for him because he was not a virgin.

Well, after falling on the floor with laughter, I explained that that is not what the text means. Once I told him that it pertains to believers who maintained their faithfulness to Christ, would you believe that he refused to accept that was the interpretation of the text? This illustrates precisely what I am saying. If you fail to grow up spiritually by first learning the ABC's of the doctrine of Christ, you will not have adequate knowledge to support your quest for obscured spiritual truths.

Another word I want to bring to your attention is "teachers" (Heb. 5:12). This word does not focus on educated people. Instead, the emphasis is on people mastering truths they learned and being able to communicate them to others. It takes time and persistent study to master particular principles of the Word.

One conclusion that we can extract from the text in Hebrews is that we are obligated to become teachers. If you do not master these basic truths, you will find it difficult to handle the meat of the Word and to have significant impact in other peoples' lives. What God does in you, should also affect others in the body of Christ. So then, without growing spiritually, you hinder yourself from proper growth as well as others. If God is delayed in developing you, others might be delayed in receiving what they need from God also. In order to make a proper contribution to the body of Christ you must grow spiritually because "every joint supplies" (Eph. 4:15, 16).

The Hebrew believers, for whatever reason, lost their lack of desire to feed; consequently, they became stagnant in their spiritual growth and, according to the writer of Hebrews, he had to teach them again the Christian ABC's. Contrary to being teachers, they were still spiritual babies. We must teach spiritual babies what is termed in Hebrews as the "elementary teachings", which are the beginning elements of the doctrine of Christ.

The apostles and prophets taught every convert to Christianity these truths in the early days of the Church. Learning from this example, we must teach every believer who becomes a Christian these basic precepts as their basis of understanding the faith.

Attempting to understand the deeper revelation from God without proper preparation through digesting this milk of the word could be catastrophic to the development of any believer. For this reason, as a pastor, I am compelled to teach these truths to our congregation once a year.

The writer to the Hebrews considered these basic principles to be "elementary [first] principles of the oracles of God (Heb. 5:12)." This refers to the Old Testament Scriptures in general (Rom. 3:1, 2; 1 Pet. 4:11). The systems established there were antitypes of what Christ would establish. Therefore, if we are to understand the elementary principles of the doctrine of Christ clearly, we must have a working knowledge of them in the Old Testament. In the following chapters then, I will examine each principle by observing how the Hebrews viewed them first then relate them to our contemporary situation.

These first principles are also the ABC's, or milk of the doctrine of Christ. There is only one other level of truth as revealed in God's word – strong meat doctrines. Consequently, there are two kinds of believers; those who are feeding on the milk of the Word and those who are feeding on the meat (1Cor. 2:6, 3:2; Heb. 5:13; 1 Pet. 2:2). Everyone begins with milk – spiritually and naturally.

Naturally, milk is the most basic form of nourishment that a mother gives to her infant, and it contains all the necessary nutrients needed for proper growth. Without the use of milk, there will be a lack of growth causing a delay in the developmental process of being able to digest strong meat.

Biblically, the word "milk" refers to those truths that are the easiest to comprehend. Anyone who has not had sufficient consumption of milk doctrines cannot receive the meat of the Word concerning Christ and his purposes. These deeper truths demand that we have the ability to chew instead of suck for digestion and nourishment. In other words, you have to be spiritually ready to do the work required to extract the nutrients that come from greater spiritual substance. To accomplish this, there must be an exercising of your spiritual faculties to continue the process of development.

The apostle Paul writes to the Corinthian believers concerning the use of milk: *"And I, brethren, could not speak to you as to spiritual men, but as to men of flesh, as to infants in Christ. I gave you milk to drink, not solid food; for you were not able to receive it. Indeed, even now you are not yet able…"* (1 Cor. 3:1, 2). Although these believers appeared to be spiritual Christians due to the abundance of the manifestation of spiritual gifts in their assemblies, their spiritual diet was yet equivalent to a baby. A spiritual "infant" is someone who is untaught as well as unskilled.

Peter gives his own sentiments concerning milk. He writes, *"Like newborn babies, long for the pure milk of the word, so that by it you may grow in respect to salvation…"* (1 Pet. 2:2). If you are in a spiritually infantile state, you must first crave the milk of the Word in order that there will be sufficient nourishment in your spirit helping you to have a healthy growth process in the Christian life.

Being on the milk of the Word is not a negative thing. It is staying on milk longer than we should that becomes problematic. A baby on milk and a 12-year-old on milk will yield two different results. While the baby would have all the nutrients they need to sustain their growth in life, the 12-year-old would develop deficiencies in their development because they should be on meat which gives them the protein, fiber, vitamins etc. for their enhancement. We must all begin with milk, but we should not remain on it.

The milk of the Word is necessary for the proper spiritual development of any believer, but how can the church continue to grow if saints never grow up spiritually?

There is something wrong with any living organism that does not develop into what nature has intended for it become. God's plan is for you to become a spiritual adult.

A pure sign that you are still a child, and the greatest hindrance to leaving milk, is a fleshly life. It does not matter how much you speak in tongues, how eloquent you are in your delivery, how much of the gifts work in your life. The manifestation of gifts is no indication of your spirituality because the gifts work by faith. All you have to do is believe that God is alive and has given you special gifts and they will begin to work. You can still be fleshly and operate your gift.

The indication of spiritual maturity is how much fruit you are bearing. How much can other people benefit from the spiritual fruit in your life? At a certain point, others should be able to advantage of what God has done in your life. However, fail to grow and you become a problem for yourself and for others who are associated with you.

The writer to Hebrews tells his audience that because they were still spiritual infants, they were unskilful in the "word of righteousness" (Heb. 5:13).

This phrase "word of righteousness" is very important because here is where you learn how to live the normal Christian life based upon the standard of righteousness, which is the single most important rule in the kingdom of God. So then, our challenge is to become spiritually mature believers in order that we may be regulated by the standard of God that is only apprehended by those who have become spiritual adults. Without being regulated by the standard of righteousness, we will not get God's best (Matt. 6:33).

Have you ever noticed that as you grew older naturally, you did not do things you did in your youth such as fight,

or talk to people however you wanted without regard for the outcome of your conversation? The older I became, the more my conduct and conversation changed. I was regulating my life by a different set of rules, such as listen first talk last. This is what the writer to the Hebrews is saying. Without sufficient spiritual development, you cannot govern your life based upon the higher laws that the meat of the Word reveals.

In contrast to milk, strong meat refers to the deeper elements concerning the doctrine of Christ. These teachings are for those who have mastered the elementary principles and have strengthened their spiritual digestive organs, through application of truth, in order to obtain a fuller knowledge of Christ. Lack of application means the lack of ability to understand instruction that has great substance. Only when you have progressed from receiving the elementary nourishment can you properly ascertain a fuller knowledge of Christ (Isa. 28:9).

Let us consider further those who are full-grown. This believer has arrived at God's ultimate goal for all His children – spiritual maturity. Through the process of habitual use in prayer, and obedience to God and His Word, these believers have developed their spiritual faculties to the place of being able to perceive that which is useful for the development of their soul.

The emphasis of the writer to the Hebrews is discerning verses knowledge gained through experience. Knowledge gained by experience alone is subject to corruption because of our fallen nature. Discerning comes from a person's spiritual capacity. Growing spiritually takes time and cannot be achieved without exercising one's spiritual senses/discernment (Heb. 5:14).

Developing your discernment is a crucial sign of your spiritual growth. Without sufficient spiritual perception, you will be susceptible to erroneous teachings (Eph. 4:14). You will most likely receive that which is good for you as well as that which is harmful (1 Jn. 4:1).

The key to developing your discernment is practice. This is what the author of Hebrews says (Heb. 5:14). He was referring to the activity of an athlete in Grecian times. These athletes employed every aspect of their being in preparation for the event they were about to be contenders in. They spent months fine-tuning their physical bodies in an attempt to achieve superiority over their competitors.

Likewise, each of us must also become spiritually fine-tuned. Daily we must exercise ourselves, developing of our spiritual awareness in order that we may prove to be superior in knowing what is useful for our inner development. Not necessarily superior to other believers, but as the athlete is finely tuned, we must condition our spirits in order to mature, as God would have it.

This practice of discerning the author wrote about pertains to those believers looking for the harmful effects of doctrine that opposes what Christ was attempting to do in their lives spiritually. They needed to listen to everything people told them about the Scriptures to make sure it was not contradicting their newfound understanding of Christ. The same is true for any believer. We must consciously listen to what people teach, ensuring that those truths do not violate the Scriptures and possibly overthrow our faith in Christ.

The profound exhortation in Hebrews is to cultivate your understanding of Christ. Since only the mature have the ability to digest deeper truths, we must press on to maturity, avoiding the repetition of these basic elements.

You have to take responsibility for your spiritual growth. God will not force you to grow. You will become spiritually mature only if you put forth the effort to do so. Unless there is cooperation between you and God concerning your spiritual growth, you will not arrive to the end that God has in mind – spiritual maturity (Eph. 4:12).

THE ABC'S

In English, ABC's are the rudiments of reading and writing or the basic components that determine our level of future learning. The better adept a child is at putting these letters together, thereby forming syllables and words, the better their reading will become, thus enabling them to move on to advanced learning.

The growing Christian must take the time to commit these principles to their memory and spirit. Without understanding theses elementary truths, it will be difficult to grow into spiritual maturity. For this reason, these precepts **must** be the first ones taught to any person coming into the Christian religion. The phrase "elementary teachings about the Christ" literally means that these are the first instructions given concerning Christ. We must not avoid this aspect of doctrine.

The ABC's consists of six elements:

1. Repentance From Dead Works

2. Faith Toward God

3. Instruction About Washings

4. Laying On Of Hands

5. The Resurrection Of The Dead

6. Eternal Judgement

In studying these six building blocks, you will gain a bird's eye view of the beginning and conclusion of the Christian faith. These basic elements will affect everything about our perception concerning Christ, his work, and if we are going to have success in ministry.

REPENTANCE FROM DEAD WORKS

We must understand and practice repentance regularly. It is a message that reverberates throughout the Old and New Covenants as an action that we must take in order to have our relationship with God restored. It is the fundamental message of both John the Baptist and Jesus (Matt. 3:2, 4:17; Luke 13:3, 5). Therefore, it must become the central thread that binds our messages together (Luke 24:47).

As we begin to consider this initial principle, we must discuss two things: repentance and dead works. Notice, the principle is **repentance** from **dead works.** A thorough examination of both elements will ensure that we comprehensively understand this element. There is a reason why this precept is leading in this series of instruction. Repentance reflects our character. Repentance shows that, as a servant of God, we are more interested in His approval of our lives than merely being workers for Him. Therefore, we must learn to have a lifestyle of repentance.

True repentance removes any hindrances in relationship/fellowship between God and man. We can expect to exemplify faith, believing God to accomplish what He desires for us only when we remove blockages from our lives. This is what repentance does for us. We will begin our consideration of this principle by defining repentance.

REPENTANCE DEFINED

Many believe that repentance is crying out to God with

tears streaming down their faces. Although this might appear as evidence in true repentance, if this external sign is the only thing present, it indicates that we merely have sorrow for what we have done. There was no true repentance. Repentance is much more than that.

The word repentance is a combination of two smaller Greek and Hebrew words. The Greek definition includes such words as **after** or **with** and refers to the way you think about something. The rest of the definition includes words like comprehension, using the mental faculties, perceiving and thinking. Therefore, repentance designates change with time coupled with a change in your perception. As you adjust your thinking, you adjust what you do in life. This is why we have to aggressively deal with every thought that contradicts the Word of God (2 Cor. 10:4, 5). Wrong thoughts negatively affect our perception. If our perception is not a Godly perception, we will not live a Godly life. If your actions do not change, you have to question the legitimacy of your repentance. If your conduct is not changing, did you really change your way of thinking?

This is why some Christians support same-sex marriage. They don't know God. If they understood God, they would know that is a strict violation of His nature and how He designed humanity. Because there is a problem with perception, there is a problem with speech. Once you change your mind and start seeing things from God's perspective, you will live a Godly life.

The Hebrew words for repentance also several meanings, such as to turn back again, to **recover** something, and also the general feeling of sorrow. While these words primarily relate to actions, there can be no doubt that change in actions will not occur unless there is a change in your mind as indicated by the emotion of sorrow.

I like the word recover. As you consider how Adam and Eve fell from their positions as rulers over this Earth, you will know that everything God is doing in the Earth through His Word, the Holy Spirit and believers is for the purpose of recovery. God's goal is to get us back to His original intent when He created Adam and Eve – dominion (Gen. 1:26). This is why the New Testament message is "repent for the kingdom of heaven is at hand" (Matt. 3:2). Repentance ultimately effects our participation in the kingdom. Christ cannot become King and Lord in our life without us first repenting (Matt. 3:2, 4:17). People must repent so that the kingdom of Christ can rule in them now and so they can occupy their place as a king in the millennial kingdom.

Repentance demonstrates that you believe God has the freedom to rule and govern your every aspect of your life. It is not enough for Jesus Christ to be Savior; he must become your Lord. As you allow him that Dominion, he will use you to impact the world. If you acknowledge His rule, you will not keep back from God what you consider to be the dearest things to you.

For example, you give up telling lies, but you will not give up your common-law marriage. You simply do not have enough revelation about God and His laws. You must strive to get closer to God by praying, fasting, reading your Bible and fellowshipping with those you know are in hot pursuit of God. The Lord cannot completely establish His kingdom in your life and use you to further it in the Earth without a lifestyle of repentance. He must rule everything about you.

Remember, the Hebrews considered repentance as

turning back to God from the thing that kept them from His blessings on their lives. They had to have a conversion in order to remain under the covenant of God. Conversion is the process of change in one's character and action. There is a shift in one's paradigm concerning the action that was being committed. This person recognizes that telling lies was sin thus; they begin to turn back to righteousness.

Finally, true repentance shows that we have resolved to live a holy life. If we continue struggling with holiness, we have not yet mastered the principle of repentance. True repentance will bring stability in your character and life as you pursue holiness with frontlets on your eyes.

Repentance affects the total man. Therefore, the definition of true repentance must be understood to produce a change in our mind, heart and actions (Matt. 9:13, 21:29; 2 Tim. 2:19).

THE FALL

Now that we have given a brief definition of repentance, let us consider why the need for it began. It all initiated with the "fall". When I write of this fall, I am referring to Adam's state of purity with God and his subsequent demise into a condition of disobedience to God.

Adam began his existence in a condition of what some theologians call "innocence". This is best described from the statement: *"And the man and his wife were both naked and were not ashamed"* (Gen. 2:25). However, at a later point in time, *"they knew they were naked"* and attempted to cover themselves (Gen. 3:7). Sin produced shame.

Before their fall from grace, Adam and Eve never experienced sin and therefore remained under the cover of

God's glory. They existed in a state of freedom from any crime against God and consequently guilt. Their lives were in complete harmony with Jehovah. God's only requirement for Adam and Eve to remain in this circumstance of innocence was to keep away from one tree, which stood in the midst of the garden, the tree of the knowledge of good and evil.

As time progressed, the war between Satan and God's creation began to ensue. After remonstrating with Eve, the Serpent prevailed, deceiving her concerning the consequences of disobeying the command of God. She partakes of this tree and offers the fruit to her husband. This atrocity culminated in Adam's disobedience. Thus, they fell from this state of innocence and for the first time, realized sin.

Because of this act of non-compliance, three things are humanity's reality until God redeems our bodies from the Earth. First, every future soul that would be born on Earth now has a sinful nature. Second, God sentenced us to physical death. Finally, there is spiritual separation from God.

BORN INTO SIN

Once Adam disobeyed God, adhering to Eve's promptings, a perpetual law was set into motion that would reverberate throughout the existence of humanity. It is called the "principle of sin" that dwells in the flesh. Sin became the primary source of influence in our lives. We do not need to teach babies how to lie, cheat and disobey. If you tell a child not to get any cookies and leave them in the room with those cookies, they will attempt to get a cookie. This is the sin principle at work in the early stages of life. Everything we do that is rebellious and evil proceeds from sin that has infused itself into our humanity. As long as we live, we will always have to address and overcome our propensity to sin.

This is why there is a constant struggle to do right. Paul, a gospel preacher, declares that the good things he desired to do, he could not while the bad things he did not want to do he did (Rom. 7:16, 17). His conclusion was that it was the effect of sin that dwelt in him. We are all subject to the same struggles. Sin will control your flesh until you are born again and have submitted your life to the Lordship of Jesus Christ.

The telltale sign that sin had entered into humanity was that Adam and Eve realized they were naked. After disobeying God, they in their shame, instinctively sewed together fig leaves to cover their nakedness (Gen. 3:7). The absence of the presence and glory of God had become a reality for them. Many describe this rebellion against God as the "original sin". Their transgression opened the door for all types of evil to exist in humankind.

These garments were insufficient to deal with the work of sin in their lives. God, in His sovereignty, made garments for them from the skin of an animal, indicating that recovery would only be possible through blood shed. This animal typified Jesus Christ. Through the shedding of the blood of Jesus, God enacted his plan to recover humanity.

Solidifying that the human race is subject to sin from birth, the great king David makes a statement that his conception was in sin (Ps. 51:5). In other words, he was born a sinner. As he grew in his mother's womb, sin infused itself into his being, developing his mind and body. Consequently, his birth was the cause of much joy and sadness. How could such an adorable, innocent baby boy do sinful things that his parents never taught him? It was sin.

The word sinner represents a state of being. It is who a person is whether they want to be or not. This infusing of sin into the human nature is the result of Adam and Eve's fall from innocence. The book of Romans clearly states that sin entered the world because of one person (Rom. 5:12). Adam passed sin on to all humankind (Rom. 5:19). Because of his disobedience, God has considered that "all have sinned". Not only are we born into this world with a disadvantage of being prone to sin but the sentence of death also awaits us.

SENTENCED TO DEATH

The entrance of sin into human nature produced death in both the physical and spiritual sense (Rom. 5:12, 14, 6:23). Spiritually, death is the loss of a consecrated life to God. Through Adam and Eve, mankind was positioned to receive His divine blessings. However, they ate from the "tree of the knowledge of good and evil" instead of the "tree of life", thus causing all of humanity to be separated from the benefits which come from having a proper relationship with God. The only way to escape this tragic situation is to receive God's work of redemption through Christ Jesus (1Cor. 1:30). While it may be difficult to grasp the concept that God imputes Adam's sin to all humankind, this remains the fact. So then, let us examine the result of humanity's undeniable ruin.

The Bible states, "...for in the day that you eat from it you will surely die" (Gen. 2:17). This is the original word from God concerning Adam and Eve's demise if they decided to rebel. Death was to be their end, and since Adam was the first human being created, the sentence of death placed in him passed on to all who would later be clothed in human flesh.

God did not mean merely an impending immediate physical death. Adam lived nine hundred and thirty years (Gen. 5:5). So then, death must have taken immediate effect in another area.

The word "die" in Genesis 2:17 refers to a death process. From the time Adam ate the fruit, he set in motion the sentence of death. He would begin dying until the process concluded in the termination of his life physically. In partaking of this tree, Adam and Eve became the forerunners of temporal (physical) as well as spiritual death.

This one uncomplicated act of disobedience ushered into the framework of humanity all the ills associated with sin. As a result, there is an open door for sin to bring humanity to a total state of depravity. Things like genocide, homosexuality, adultery, fornication, strife, theft, extortion, idolatry, sickness, drunkenness and partying leading to all kinds of debauchery has become the social order of our day, precisely demonstrating the need for repentance (1Cor. 6:9, 10; Gal. 5:19-21).

Thank God that He did not leave us in this condition but provided a way out – Jesus Christ who died on the cross, paying penalty for Adam's indiscretion. Jesus became our way to escape death both spiritually and physically.

ALIENATED FROM THE LIFE OF GOD

According to Ephesians chapter four verses seventeen and eighteen, we see that this death became an alienation from God's divine and perfect life. *"So this I say, and affirm together with the Lord, that you walk no longer just as the Gentiles also walk, in the futility of their mind, being darkened in their understanding, excluded from the life of God because of the ignorance that is in them, because of the hardness of their heart...*"

Our natural mind-set is one that is prone to rejecting knowledge concerning God because our every thought is filled with the knowledge of sin and wickedness (Rom. 1:21; James 3:19). In short, we live according to the "futility of [our] mind." Thoughts of perversion and corruption pervade every psyche. This is the condition of everyone apart from redemption through Christ.

Futility or "vanity" is extremely apparent in our society. All we have to do is watch the commercials that sell all types of products through means of sexual implications. Music videos promote fast money, men having multiple women etc. Humanity lives in the "futility of their minds" and is ignorant about God (Jer. 2:5).

People's ignorance is not due to God keeping Himself hidden but because they reject what He reveals about Himself and His nature. The people of the world have intentionally hardened their hearts through the willful and habitual practice of rejecting spiritual truth, which is the cause of separation from fellowship with God through his Divine life (2 Kgs. 17:14, 15; John 3:19, 20; Rom. 1:21).

When a minister is preaching a message to people in a congregation in an attempt to help them become more like God and deal with life's issues, and they sit with their arms folded as to say "I'm really not listening to you I'm just here", and then leave church and began to do the things that are contrary to what God has revealed about Himself, that is a sign of willful ignorance.

The word "hardness" in Ephesians means "a hardening of the external". The conscience of man became callous towards what is right. Humanity has hardened their will and emotions toward God (Mark 3:5). The reason why people will not repent is because they have hardened their heart. That's why they will make statements such as "I don't want to hear what you have to say", "My soul is okay without you" and "I'm not interested in your religion." These statements represent a hardening of the external, which perpetuates the separation in spiritual life.

God's original intent for man was to exist with eternal life in its abundance (John 10:10). Accordingly, He placed in Eden the tree of the knowledge of good and evil and the tree of life. If Adam had partaken of the tree of life, he would have gained eternal life. Instead, he alienated himself from eternal life. Now God is in the process of restoring people.

As long as a person remains alienated from God's divine life, there remains the sentence of death upon them, *"For the wages of sin is death..."* (Rom. 6:23). The only guarantee sin can give to every human being is death. This death is both physical and spiritual.

WE MUST REPENT

Even though the sentence of death is upon all of humanity, the love that God has for us caused Him to make a way of escape from this penalty. Not all was lost with Adam's rebellion. God will still accomplish His initial purpose for creating man; He just used an alternative route – Jesus. Now God commands us to repent in order to become beneficiaries of what his Son accomplished.

The apostle Paul uses the strongest language writing, *"Therefore having overlooked the times of ignorance, God is now **declaring** to men that all people everywhere should* *repent...*"(Acts 17:30). Repenting is not an option if we wish to escape the evils brought about by the sin element in humanity and its subsequent judgement because of them.

The word "ignorance" has the same meaning contained in Ephesians 4:18. It is ignorance of spiritual realities. The greatest ignorance that anyone can have is that of God and His nature. I would hasten to remind you that this is man's willful ignorance of God and divine things.

Since we see that ignorance plays such an important role in the void between God and man, it is easy to conclude that man sins because he does not know God. This could be true for some believers who claim they are walking in the Way; yet, have spotted lives due to indulgence in gross sin (1 Thes. 4:4, 5).

Paul says that before the redemptive work of Christ, God overlooked this ignorance; however, He is now (through his messengers) ordering every person to live a life indicative of abhorring sin (Acts 14:16). God is not accepting ignorance about spiritual truths any longer. He is commanding repentance.

The word "declaring" indicates that there are no exceptions to the rule. This must happen either to avoid certain events or to qualify for others (Jer. 7:3-5, 26:3; Amos 5:4-6). According to this passage in the book of Acts, God requires repentance to help us escape the immediate judgement that Christ will bring upon the world when he returns (Acts 17:31). Make no mistake about it, the Earth and everything in it will undergo judgement.

The extent of this command is to "all people" and "everywhere". Hence, people in every locality, as God's subjects, are required to repent. Who can escape this declaration? Do not think that you are wiser than God, lest the end time bring upon you experiences God never intended for you to have.

There are two things God gave people which make it possible for him to command repentance. These are a divine revelation of Himself and the redemptive work of his Son. No one can say he or she did not know God. Where there is no preacher declaring the gospel, there is creation testifying to the reality of God (Rom. 1:18-20).

In addition, God sent his Son to give man an opportunity for everyone to repent and be recovered (John 3:16). These provisions make it impossible for humanity to have any excuses as to why they did not repent.

At this point you might be asking yourself, "Will God automatically forgive people who intentionally premeditate sin, carry it out with the attitude that I will simply repent later?" "Is God at every person's beck and call that He will grant repentance merely because they ask?" "Won't this type of disposition give individuals license to sin?" Well, let us continue and consider another aspect of repentance.

REPENTANCE MUST BE GRANTED

God has to grant repentance to a person. True repentance will take place only if there is an outpouring of grace in a person's spirit coupled with them realizing their need to repent. If these two conditions do not synchronize like musicians in an orchestra playing a piece that Beethoven wrote, there will be no repentance.What does it mean for God to grant repentance? Let us consider an episode in the life of the apostle Peter to begin our inquiry. In Acts chapter ten, we find Peter receiving a life and message altering

REPENTANCE FROM DEAD WORKS

revelation from God.

On one particular day, he was on the rooftop of a house and began praying. Around noon, Peter became hungry. God took this opportunity to give Peter a vision of animals, creatures and birds (Acts 10:12). Peter had a problem with this vision. According to the Mosaic Law, it was unlawful for Jews to eat any beast considered unclean (Lev. 11:4-7, 19-20).

The Lord tells Peter to kill these animals and make a meal. However, Peter would not. The apostle to the Jews responded by declaring that he has never eaten anything that was unlawful for a Jew to eat (Acts 10:14).The Lord makes a final statement to him concerning this vision. God tells Peter not to consider the things made holy by Him as unholy. As Peter pondered what this meant, he would soon come to realize that this vision would pertain to the Gentiles coming into the faith. Peter realized God's plan for the ages. The Lord granted repentance to the Gentiles along with the Jews (Acts 5:31, Eph. 2:12-18).

As he continued to ponder this vision, three men approached him sent by a man named Cornelius, a centurion, a just man requesting Peter to come with them (10:28, 34-35). The apostle, perceiving God's revelation, returned with them to Cornelius' house understanding that God was opening the door of salvation to the Gentiles. This in effect was God granting repentance to the uncircumcised through Peter.

The conclusion of the story shows us that Cornelius and his household glorified God after the apostle preached saying, *"...Well then, God has granted to the Gentiles also the repentance that leads to life"*(Acts 11:18). Indeed, God has granted repentance to all humanity through the redemptive work of Christ. However, this pertains unto all men believing in Christ Jesus for salvation. To put it another way, God has granted "repentance unto life".

God must also continue to grant repentance to those who sin after salvation. Only the foolish decide willfully to sin assuming that God will allow them to repent later.

Jesus makes a profound declaration, shedding further light on this issue. He states that men have to be drawn to him through the efficacious prompting of God (John 6:44). Without God doing the drawing, a person will not come to seek salvation in Jesus Christ. Our Savior knew that no one would commit himself or herself to his instruction, entering into fellowship with him, without the Father's drawing him or her.

The word "draw" speaks of leading a person to come to Jesus because of an inward compelling. Again, we see two elements at work: God working inwardly in an individual to impel them to come and the person willfully choosing to come.The fact that God works to bring inward prompting is the work of grace allowing people to receive the gracious gift that God is offering them. We must not lack such knowledge as to understand that we cannot rashly commit offenses against God presumptuously believing that He will allow us to repent afterward.Paul penned this very thing to the Romans. These individuals refused to acknowledge God in their actions. Instead, they willing continued to commit offenses against God. Consequently, He failed to grant them repentance; rather, allowing the things they desired to consume them (Rom. 1:21-31).

As Paul continued to write, he later indicated that God leads people to repentance (Rom. 2:4). What does this mean? Despite a person's repeated provocations against God, He continues to forgive the many crimes and offenses against Him, showing that He desires that all would experience salvation (2 Pet. 3:9). Therefore, in accordance to His kindness, He leads men to repent.

Paul's words coincide with those of our Lord's. To "lead" is to "draw". At the precise time, God moves inwardly to inspire one to repent. Like the conductor of a symphony, He methodically supervises the heart helping it to become harmonious with the working of the Holy Spirit who prompts repentance within it. Paul had a profound understanding of this. Although God is longsuffering and forbearing, the continuance in sin will result eventually in retribution from Him.

In conclusion, we must consider a text that the apostle Paul also penned to Timothy, his son in the gospel. This advocate of Christ writes that individuals who are servants of God must deal with those who oppose the gospel and their heretical knowledge as peaceful persons. He exhorts his spiritual son not to argue with these individuals, but with humility correct them *"...if perhaps God may grant them repentance..."* (2 Tim. 2:25). God has to **grant** repentance to everyone.

One key word of interest in this verse is "if". This means that repentance is not automatically given. There is uncertainty as to whether someone will see the error of his or her ways. Let us conduct our days with all soberness knowing that the grace we have in our lives to repent is a gift given by God in accordance with His providence.

REPENTANCE FOR SAVED VS. UNSAVED PEOPLE

When considering this topic on repentance, we must categorize the way that repentance must be completed based upon the individual we are referring to. We need to examine if they are a believer or not. It can be quite simple to understand whom the Scripture is alluding to based upon the context.

Simply put, believers repent of sins (plural) while unsaved people repent of sin (singular). The result of repentance also differs for these two groups. Let us consider the process of repentance for believers first.

According to John's first epistle, it is the confession of our **sins** that is applicable to the believer. The verse states, *"If we confess our **sins**, He is faithful and righteous to forgive us our **sins** and to cleanse us from all unrighteousness"* (1 Jn. 1:9).

For the observant people who would say that sin is in the singular in verses seven and eight, I would concur with them. These two statements in the first epistle of John *"cleanses us from all sin"* and *"If we say that we have no sin"* indeed show sin in the singular form; however, sin is different in those contexts. The emphasis is on a single act of sin instead of continuous acts. The text is merely showing us that sinful acts remain problematic even for believers. Yet sin must not become so evident in our lives that we cannot remember when we have sinned.

The remedy for a believer who has sinned is confession of that particular deed. In doing this, the writer says that God will forgive them of this deed and will apply the blood of Jesus, by sprinkling it upon their conscience, thereby delivering them from the guilt of this sin also (1 Jn. 1:7; Ezek. 36:25; Heb. 10:22).

Believers need to repent of their sins not to gain relationship with God but to restore fellowship with Him (1 Kgs. 8:47-50; 1 Jn. 1:3). Relationship never ceases once God redeems an individual. However, there is a rift in fellowship when sin is present because God is a holy God (Matt. 27:46).

Imagine you have three children. Two of them live with you and enjoy all the benefits of their fellowship with you. The other has left the house, committed murder, and is now serving a life sentence without the possibility of parole. Though you will never be able to have true fellowship with him again, he is still your son. He will never stop being your son because of his bloodline. Sin impedes our fellowship with God even though we may be His children. This was the case with the prodigal son. He did not sever relationship with his father; rather, their fellowship was broken (Luke 15:11ff).

By contrast, unbelievers repent of **sin** not **sins**. A look into the gospel of John will affirm this point. Jesus speaks concerning the work of the Spirit stating, *"And He, when He comes, will convict the world concerning sin and righteousness and judgement; concerning **sin**, because they do not believe in Me..."* (John 16:8, 9). The only thing that causes the Lord to confine the unbelieving portion of humanity to eternal perdition is their **sin** (singular). Repentance brings sinners into relationship with God, which is His primary objective. For the unbeliever, they repent unto salvation (Matt. 9:13). Some may prefer the term "getting saved". The only thing that unbelievers need to repent of is their failure to believe in Christ (Rom. 10:8, 9).

After the ascension of our Lord, he released to his disciples the Holy Spirit who would accomplish several tasks. One of those tasks is to convict the world of their sin. This can only happen in two distinct ways. First, He will convict the world through the life and words of other believers. Second, the Holy Spirit himself will move in the heart of the unbeliever.

Because the Lord is interested in the conviction of sinners, we must make sure our lives as believers are on point as concerns our walk with God. For those who have not yet been born again, you and I will become the conviction they need in order for them to exemplify a turn-a-round in their lives through placing their faith in Jesus Christ as they repeat the "sinner's prayer".

I have heard many preachers lead people in this prayer. Usually somewhere in this recital, they have those who desire to be saved make a statement asking God to forgive them of their sins (deeds). This is not Biblical. According to the gospel of John, the only thing that condemns a person to eternal damnation is the sin of unbelief. It is not their sins which send them to the lake of fire although they will be judged for these deeds (John 8:24).

John states, *"He who believes in Him is not judged; he who does not believe has been judged already, because he has not believed in the name of the only begotten Son of God"* (John 3:18). This is a continuation of the famous salvation scripture of John 3:16. If you gaze at this text, you will see that only unbelief in the name of Jesus Christ condemns a person to eternal damnation. That's it, that's all (John 1:12).

Simply put, unbelievers send themselves to the lake of fire. It is not God's doing. He has made the provision for everyone to escape this judgement – Jesus Christ. The repentant one simply needs to project their faith unto Jesus Christ, believing that he is the author of eternal salvation in the kingdom of God (Mark 16:16; Rom. 10:8, 9).

My point is simplistic. Believers repent of their unrighteous deeds while sinners repent of their unbelief in

Jesus Christ. If we understand this, we will address these two groups of individuals properly and without confusion.

HOW GOD BRINGS PEOPLE TO REPENTANCE

You might ask, "What are some of the things that bring individuals to repentance?" This is a great question. God uses different methods for different situations. If you go to Africa on a missionary journey, to preach Jesus to the natives, you must demonstrate the power of God more than the revelation of God. Before you can preach Jesus to them, you have to show their tribe that Jesus can heal them. If you're among intellectuals, you have to intellectualize with them concerning the gospel. God's is not confined to using one method. There are at least six factors God uses to bring believers and unbelievers to repentance.

The way He deals with His mature children is through spiritual chastisement. When God disciplines, He does so with the intent to produce righteousness in the lives of His children (Heb. 12:4-11). Again, this is only for the spiritually mature, who can discern in their spirit that God is dealing with them. The immature saint will not know this is God dealing with them. When things go wrong, they will be quick to blame it on the Devil, not knowing that God is actually trying to get them to return to righteousness.

The word "discipline" in Hebrews literally means "to flog" (Heb. 12:6). In modern day vernacular, we call this a "beating". God uses situations to beat His children in order that they may turn to Him again and align themselves with holiness. Although this is painful, our Father permits it because He loves us.

One of the greatest methods that God uses to bring a

person to repentance is preaching. Romans 10:8-14 is perhaps one of the most well-known Bible verses about repentance. Sinners are able to make a confession of repentance and express belief in Jesus Christ because God sent a preacher to them, who inspired faith in their life after he delivered a message about believing in Jesus Christ (vs. 8). This aspect of ministering is not for a select few.

You might be saying to yourself, "I'm not a preacher." I have news for you, we are all ministers of Christ; consequently, we must all preach repentance (2 Cor. 5:18, 19). Every redeemed child of God has the word and ministry of reconciliation. I'm not talking about being licensed, or ordained. I'm talking about who you are as a believer. If God has saved you, you have the responsibility to talk to others about Jesus Christ.

This is why it behoves us to watch how we live. We directly impact how people perceive Christ through how they perceive Christ in us. If people wrongly perceive him in us because of how we are living, that has a negative impact on our message. If our message is corrupted, how can we inspire anyone's faith? Consequently, they will tell you they don't want anything to do with Jesus because he has not shown himself visible in your life.

God also uses miracles and other mighty acts to cause people to repent. Matthew writes about Jesus rebuking the cities where he did most of his mighty works. Despite seeing those acts, the people who lived in those cities would not repent. Jesus makes the declaration to Chorazin and Capernaum that those who resided in Tyre, Sidon and Sodom would have repented had they seen those same mighty deeds (Matt. 11:20-24).

This statement shows two things. One, God will do

whatever He has to do to bring people to repentance. He would work whatever miracles necessary to ensure that you place your faith in His son Jesus. This also says to us that we cannot be worried about who repents and who does not. The results are up to God. Our job is to be a conduit for God to use however He wishes.

Godly sorrow is also a tool that God uses (2 Cor. 7:10). This is grieving to the extent that we are willing to align ourselves with the will of God in order to please Him, resulting in an improved spiritual condition represented by our turning away from sinful actions. We will not become truly repentant unless there is godly sorrow.

We cannot overlook God's goodness. Paul's epistle to the Romans states that God's goodness or kindness causes men to repent (Rom. 2:4). God shows His goodness through His kindness towards us. While He could have judged us, His mercy has shown itself superior to judgement (James 2:13). This does not mean that men should remain unrepentant. There is a time that judgement will prevail (1 Pet. 4:17). God is longsuffering and kind towards all men because He desires to see all humanity come to repentance (2 Pet. 3:9). The Lord has an immense desire to recover all who would believe in Christ Jesus because He longs to have fellowship with us.

Finally, God brings people to repentance through His warnings. Throughout the history of Israel, we see them continuously rebelling against God, turning towards idolatry, marrying those they were warned not to and practicing many social injustices. They violated many of the ordinances that Moses gave them (Isa. 1:18-20; Jer. 1:14-16; Zeph. 2:1-3).

God gave them warnings on many occasions that if their

behavior did not change, He would put them into bondage to other nations. As we observe their legacy, due to Israel's incessant sin, we see that ultimately, the Assyrians and Babylonians executed the judgement of God when they captured Israel.

Similarly, in the New Testament, God gives a multiplicity of warnings to His children. The Revelation of John contains several warnings directed to the churches of Asia Minor. He warns the people of the Church of Ephesus to return to their first love (Rev. 2:4, 5). Another warning is contained within the message to the Church of Pergamos. They were full of false doctrines, which would include those of Balaam and the Nicolaitans (Rev. 2:14-16). Warnings reflect the patience of God and His desire to withhold judgement from those that He loves.

THE BENEFITS OF REPENTANCE

Everyone wants benefits. People who sell homes are trained to tell their customers about the benefits of the house they are selling. People who sell cars they tell you about the benefits of purchasing that particular automobile. They will tell you that their automobile gets 42 miles per gallon; the makers have redesigned it and it has a larger interior than the previous model. Why do you think is God any different? He knows that as humans we look for benefits. Consider even a simple thing like marriage.

I married my wife because of the benefits that she offered along with her love. She loved God, she was a great mother and she was fun to be around. If she could not have offered me the things that I was looking for in life, I would not have married her. We do things because we gain benefits. There are benefits that come into your life because you repent.

Probably the most important benefit would be forgiveness (Luke 24:47). Again, God forgives sin and sins (see discussion of repentance for believers vs. unbelievers). Jesus makes this statement in Luke, *"...unless you repent, you will all likewise perish"*(Luke 13:3).These words did not merely predict the destruction of Jerusalem, but also pointed to the dreadful day of the Lord in which he would return to exact judgement upon all humankind.

In the book of Acts, people were amazed at how Peter was able to help a man who was crippled his entire life, receive healing from God. The apostle began to preach what would become a great message to the Jews about their Messiah.

God has sent him to Earth to be an appeasement for our sins. Instead of receiving him as the Messiah, they denied and crucified him (This was all in the plan of God). Peter concludes his sermon with these words, *"Therefore repent and return, so that you sins may be wiped away, in order that the times of refreshing may come from the presence of the Lord"* (Acts 3:19). Upon their turning to God in reformation, He would erase their sins. These repentant ones would experience refreshing now, also when Christ returns to reign in his state of blessedness.

When a sinner repents, they have restored relationship with God. Their life instantly becomes a paradox because they are now in two places at once (Eph. 2:5-7). God unites us with His son in heaven showing that He intends for believers to experience all the graciousness that Christ will bestow upon his loyal disciples (Eph. 1:2). At the same time, He resides in us by His Spirit.

The Lord gives the Holy Ghost to repentant ones. As we refer back to Acts, Peter is again preaching to the Israelites concerning the Lordship of Christ (Acts 2:37-41). When the day of Pentecost had come, people began speaking in other national languages which they had no formal training (Acts 2:6). While those listening were astonished, Peter began to preach. At the conclusion of his message, he told them if they repent, they could receive this same gift (Acts 2:38). This gift was promised by Jesus and was to be received after his ascension (John 15:16-19). Everyone who repents, gaining restored relationship with Christ can receive this gift. Both the sin of unbelief and sin (deeds) will hinder one from receiving this precious gift.

Repentant people gain God's favor. This is His approval of their lives as well as a gracious participation in it. He will treat them tenderly even when they find themselves in difficult scenarios because they refused to obey Him initially.

In chapter twenty-six of Leviticus, Moses speaks to the Israelites regarding the blessings of obedience. In verses nine and eleven, there are two statements which stand out, *"I will turn toward you"* and *"My soul will not reject you."* Moses writes that if the Israelites maintain unshakable obedience to God, He will establish them; consequently, solidifying their fellowship with Him.

The benefits of this fellowship would be incomparable. They would be fruitful, abounding in every way (vs. 9). Even more so, God would establish His covenant with them. He would also live amongst them (vs. 11). This is His favor.

After verse thirteen, Moses shows them the punishments that will come because of disobedience. However, God is faithful to His children. Although they will find themselves in thorny situations, if they repent, they will again gain God's attention. He will remember His covenant to the father of all who believe – Abraham. God will bless Israel in the land of their captivity. His favor would culminate in ruthless judgement upon those nations that He used to bring His people into captivity (2 Chr. 7:14, 15; Hosea 14:2,4ff).

The Scripture promises healing to those who repent (James 5:14-16). The responsibility of an elder when praying for a sick person is to anoint them with oil and speak a prayer of faith. However, the sick person will not experience healing unless he or she confesses that they have deviated from the truth and uprightness.

These verses in the epistle of James are indicating that this particular sickness is due to sin. Unless there is repentance of transgression, sickness will remain an active enemy in the body of the believer. Therefore, *"...the effective prayer of a righteous man can [not] accomplish much."* Despite a great prayer of faith, you and I will not obtain healing if we do not repent of sin.

Our prayers will be heard by God (2 Chr. 7:14). When Solomon was dedicating the temple through prayer, he alluded to the impending acts of disobedience and sin that Israelites would commit. However, Solomon beautifully appeals the God to "hear from heaven" in response to their change in attitude and action (2 Chr. 6:22-27).

After the king's intense supplication, the Lord appeared unto him. In His promise to Solomon He states that the individuals who humble themselves in prayer will gain the eye and ear of God (2 Chr. 7:14, 15). You will have His attention and favor.

We gain access into the kingdom of God (John 3:1-5). This is the greatest benefit that God wants to give us. There was a Pharisee, named Nicodemus, who approached Jesus on a particular night, speaking to him concerning the miracles he performed. Jesus responds to his statements indicating that these events happen in the kingdom of God.

He further states two particulars. If one wants to **see** this kingdom of God, he must experience a new birth conversion. This is repentance. To see is merely to partake of salvation in the kingdom of God. This is the first step.

Secondly, there must be baptism to **enter** the kingdom of God. Many theologians have debated concerning what this baptism is. Some say it is baptism by water (Matt. 3:2). Others say it is the baptism of the Holy Spirit (Acts 1:5). Whatever your interpretation is, one thing is for sure, there must also be baptism to enjoy the kingdom of God which is to be a present and future possession of believers (Matt. 4:17; Mark 1:15; 2 Pet. 1:8-11).

Repentance also allows us to enjoy Christ. In John's Revelation, he relates Christ's word to the Church of Laodicea concerning their lackluster desire for fellowship with the Lord (Rev. 3:14-22). Although they maintained an over-confidence concerning their spiritual wealth, they needed to repent. Christ Jesus exhorts them stating, *"Behold, I stand at the door and knock; if anyone hears My voice and opens the door, I will come in to him and will dine with him, and he with Me"* (Rev. 3:20).

Some expositors view this as a metaphor for intimate fellowship. Others believe it refers to Christ's second coming. Both perspectives have merit. The point is clear that Christ desires repentance in order to have intimate fellowship and enjoyment with his people.

The great statement here is "will dine with him". This means that Christ will enable believers to have close intimate fellowship with him. This is the ultimate expression that Christ can give based upon your repentance (Rev. 3:14-22). We can have great anticipation about this intense time of future fellowship.

THE PROCESS OF REPENTANCE

Upon examining the benefits of repentance, someone might be ready to repent. For the seasoned in Christ, this might be elementary. However, for the young in the faith, they may be asking, "How do I truly repent?" At this point, I invite you to observe the following steps to ensure that you obtain true repentance.

First, it is impossible to repent without the acknowledgment of sin. To acknowledge your sin is perhaps the most difficult part of the process. Sometimes we avoid confronting our failure. Nevertheless, this is where the rubber meets the road. In this initial step you come to terms with the fact that you have offended God and possibly others.

What does it mean to acknowledge your sin? It merely means to confess it. Psalm chapter fifty-one gives us a detailed look into the process of repentance from one of God's mighty men, King David. He writes this psalm after the prophet Nathan confronted him for stealing Bath-sheba, Uriah's wife.

If you are unaware of the story I will capsulate it for you. Israel was fighting a war. As their chief-in-commander, David should have been leading them. Instead, he remained in Jerusalem. In the evening, he takes a walk on his roof and sees a woman taking a bath. Her beauty becomes a delight to his eyes. After diligently inquiring about her, he found out that she was the wife of a man named Uriah, a dedicated soldier David's army.

Showing his selfishness and greed, David had Uriah sent to the front of the military line knowing that he would be killed. Upon receiving news that Uriah was dead, David married Bath-sheba. This was one of his greatest sins (2 Sam. 11:1ff). It is from this context that David writes Psalm 51.

In this prayer we find David asking God for forgiveness and purging. During his process of repenting he makes a powerful statement, *"For I know my transgressions, And my sin is ever before me"* (Ps. 51:3). This was the acknowledgement that his sin haunts him day and night. He was not happy. This is what I mean when I say this is perhaps the most painful step in the process (Ps. 38:3-8, 18).

Your life might be ensnared because of a bad decision, but if you want to truly repent, you must confront it dealing with God and possibly man. I pray that you would have the humility and courage to come face to face with your sin. This step consequently leads to the second. Confronting your sin will lead to Godly sorrow.

Godly sorrow speaks of your mental anguish for what you have done. David's thoughts relentlessly reminded him about his indiscretion. Godly sorrow shows that you recognize that you have violated God's laws.

This painful process must be accompanied by action because *"sorrow that is according to the will of God produces a repentance without regret..."* (2 Cor. 7:10). Painful regret of our sin leads us to work out our salvation via repentance; thus, the repentance process culminates in this final step.

A transformed life demonstrates true repentance. This is visibly forsaking sin. The epistle of James deals with a particular issue of "faith and works" (James 2:17, 18). Although this passage pertains to providing for the necessity of our brothers and sisters, I desire to show that we must demonstrate our faith for repentance by action. Your actions define your faith. If you say you had faith to repent, then altered actions should proceed because faith cannot be deemed valid unless there are proper indicators – actions (James 2:20, 26).

I am not advocating that if a person's actions have not changed, they never truly repented. I am merely suggesting that your repentance may become questionable to those who are looking for a change in your behavior.

John the Baptist had this same outlook. As he preached in the desert, there were those who scoffed at his message. He tells them to bring something to him, showing a sign of their repentance (Matt. 3:8). A change in a person's actions indicates a change in their heart and mind. This is the most obvious way to demonstrate that you have reconsidered your ways. The difficult thing here is to establish new habits, but God's grace is sufficient to help every person establish actions indicative of their repentance (Matt. 11:20-21; Luke 3:8; Acts 19:18, 19; 26:20).

As we can see here, repentance is not a difficult task. Following these steps will change your life. Repentance will enable you to align yourself with the will and ways of God; thereby becoming pleasing to Him.

ELIMINATING DEAD WORKS

Now that we have discussed repentance at length, let us consider dead works. Remember our principle states, *"Repentance from **dead works**"* (Heb. 6:1). Every action, whether good or bad, that does not emanate from the divine life of God is a dead work (Heb. 9:14). Dead works fail to gain God's approval and will cause you to lose any possible rewards at the judgement seat of Christ. If it's a good thing and not a God thing then it's a dead thing.

We can observe dead works from two paradigms. They are those done **before** salvation in an effort to obtain it and those done **after** salvation in an effort to please God (Isa. 64:6; 1 Cor. 3:12-14; Heb. 11:6). In either case, the emphasis is on a person doing something considered good by themselves or another individual but dead by God. Lifeless works are proof that we are trusting in ourselves to obtain righteousness and rewards instead of grace which comes from divine life operating in us (Rom. 10:3; Philip. 3:9).

If someone says that they help keep the church clean by dusting and taking out the trash, and continues to live their life as a heathen, they have done a good thing but not a God thing. Consequently, it is a dead thing. Any action that does not derive from the life of God is a dead work. So then, outside of repenting and gaining restored relationship with God, everything a person does is a dead work. Until God saves you, it does not matter how much money you give to the church, how much you feed the hungry or help pay someone's light bill, it may be a good work but it is a dead work because it does not emanate from the life of God.

People will like you, thank you and even give you praise, but when God looks at what you did, He considers it a dead work. You may be called to do some of these things, but until there is divine life in you, none of what you do has any eternal value at the judgement seat of Christ.

Repentance from dead works helps us to have a new point of origin from which we live. The issue is to begin living a spiritual life. There has to be an adjustment in how you view the life of God before you can be profitable to God. Such an adjustment cannot be made until there is application to our lives of the blood of Christ through repentance. This is the only way to produces works that are eternally productive; thus, pleasing to God. As we live our lives conscious of repenting from dead works, we guarantee ourselves of God's approval and every reward that our lives have gained.

The only thing required to obtain salvation is faith. However, when it comes to gaining rewards, the way we live our lives will determine what God gives to us. The more productive we are, the greater our reward will be because He gives us what we earn through the life we have lived (Matt. 25:14ff; Luke 19:11ff; 1Cor. 3:12-15).

Jesus did not perform any dead works. He explicitly made the statement that he did not do anything of himself. He only did what he perceived the Father doing (John 5:19). It is imperative for us to become cognizant of Jesus' life effort.

We must live our lives based upon what God has determined us to do (John 7:16, 8:28). The only way to escape dead works is to understand what God is calling you to do. Consequently, you must spend time with Him to understand what He wants. As you perform only the tasks which God wants you to do, you make sure that every work is a good work. You do not have to live life demonstrating **dead** works, on the contrary, you are capable and mandated to accomplish **good** works (Eph. 2:10, Col. 1:10).

LIVING IN DELIVERANCE

I have shown the importance and necessity of repentance. It was a message heralded by John the Baptist, Jesus, his disciples, the apostles and should be by you and me. Repentance will invariably lead to a vibrant lifestyle of faith towards God. Throughout the ages, we must continue to preach this message of "repentance from dead works".

We need to live in deliverance after repenting. We live in deliverance through the blood of Jesus, who purges our conscience from "dead works" in order that we may serve God. (Heb. 9:14).

So, repentance from dead works is God's goal for every person. Through this process we change the way we view God, His nature and consequently life; thereby, enabling us to become productive believers.

FAITH TOWARD GOD

Repentance towards God must be coupled with the reality of faith towards Jesus Christ (Acts 20:21). Preaching repentance without preaching faith towards Jesus Christ is like a physician who makes a surgical incision down the middle of someone's body to deal with the cause of sickness, but neglects to stitch them back together to bring their complete healing. Repentance is only half the process of recovery.

If there is no forward momentum after you have repented you have only gone half the distance. Half the distance of a football field will not give you a score if you start from one-yard line. You cannot win a race if you only run half of it. Faith will take you through the second half of the distance.

Faith is a subject that became the foundation for the belief system of the Hebrews. Early in the pages of history, Abel presented a sacrifice to God because he believed in Him (Gen. 4:4; Heb. 11:4). Others exhibited faith towards God to accomplish the most amazing feats and to endure the brutal trials they experienced. In fact, the eleventh chapter of Hebrews is a testimony of the unwavering faith of the people of God. Faith must become a reality in our lives if we are going to have the testimony borne to us that we are well pleasing to God (Heb. 11:6).

THE NEED FOR FAITH

Scripture is clear, *"And without faith it is impossible to please Him, for he who comes to God must believe that He is and that He is a rewarder of those who seek Him"* (Heb. 11:6). Faith is indispensable to having a life that pleases God. Faith sees the end from the beginning. Faith is the motivation for action. Faith in God is the element that gives you stability when there are storms in your life. God does not want our motivation to come from what we feel and see primarily but what we believe.

FAITH IS COMMANDED

In the principle of repentance from dead works, we observed that repentance is commanded (Acts 17:30). Well, God also commands that we have faith by believing in the name of Jesus (1 Jn. 3:23a). This is the only instance where the Bible commands us to have faith. Any other time Scripture speaks about faith, it is in conditional terms. This is why Jesus made statements such as, "**If** you have faith", "**If** you believe" or "**Only** believe" (Matt. 17:20, 21:22; Mark 5:36; Luke 17:6).

The reason why God commands us to believe in the name of Jesus is because believing in his name is equivalent to believing in him and all that he has accomplished on our behalf. This is what separates Christianity from other religions. While others believe that Christ merely walked the Earth as a man, we believe in him for salvation.

If we remain fully persuaded about whom he is and what he has done, we can have faith for everything else. Without believing in him first, there is no valid basis for believing that he can help with any other aspect of our lives.

FAITH DEFINED

So what is faith exactly? Actually, it has several connotations. The word faith in Hebrews 6:1 has three areas, which become of primary importance to us as we discuss faith toward God, (1) we must be convinced of the reality of God's existence, (2) we must be persuaded that He is the creator and ruler of all things, and (3) we must believe that He gives eternal salvation through Christ. From this perspective, our faith introduces us to the beginning of who God is to the conclusion of what He will do.

Adding to this, we can examine the notable scripture used to define faith found in Hebrews 11:1. *"Now faith is the assurance of things hoped for, the conviction of things not seen."* This is a very valid scripture to help obtain a beginning definition of faith; yet it is insufficient to gain an exhaustive description because faith is only described in terms that are fitting with the context of what is being written about – promises (Heb. 11:6, 39, 40). However, we can start here.

Notice, faith becomes the substance of your hope. The reader with the vigilant eye will observe that faith is **the** assurance of what you hope for.

The word "the" is different from the word "an". Faith is **the** assurance not **an** assurance. There is no other avenue to give credence to your anticipation for some future thing or event other than faith.

The next word to observe is assurance. This word actually means to stand under. Faith becomes the platform for confidence. It makes the promises of God firm and an inner reality in your life. Without faith as a foundation, there will be no visible manifestation of what is unseen (Heb. 11:6, 8, 13, 24ff).

The things hoped for in the strictest sense here are the things which the individuals in this chapter sought after. These "things" include the New Jerusalem (vs. 10), Sarah's seed (vs. 11), the reward (vs. 26), a better resurrection (vs. 35) and the promise (vs. 39). If we applied the "things hoped for" in our present context, it would be the things which are contained in the Word of God as well as what He has spoken into your spirit.

The word faith also includes the following definitions: It is the conviction of a particular truth, a belief that Jesus is the Messiah and the persuasion of things lawful for a Christian. Subjectively, it is the acknowledgment of divine things whereas objectively, it is the substance of Christian faith or the principles that define the Christian system of belief.

THE OBSTACLE TO FAITH

There is one main obstacle to faith – sin. This is the root cause of doubt. The reason why some saints cannot believe God for anything is because of the presence of sin. Sin is counterproductive to faith (Rom. 14:23). Even though God commands us to have faith, to continue growing in it requires us living in a way that conforms to the righteous standard of God.

FAITH MUST HAVE AN OBJECT

There is no such thing as blind faith. Everyone has faith in something or someone. Faith must have an object. What does this mean? Faith must be projected somewhere. It must be validated by something. So your faith is only as strong as the object that validates it. If I place my faith in my wife, it can be shaken because my wife, as a human, has weaknesses. However, if I place my faith in an unchanging immoveable God, then my faith has the ability to remain strong when everything around me is being shaken as if in a hurricane.

In the Bible there are certain elements which faith has as a focus. These are God, Christ, the Law, the Prophets, the gospel and God's promises. The reality of these objects gives your faith its validity.

God is the ultimate object of faith since He is the source of all things (John 14:1). The scripture states, *"... believe in God, believe also in Me."* Some people believe this statement is in the imperative form. They believe that Jesus is commanding his followers to believe in him. This could also be interpreted as a question as if Jesus was asking them, "Do you believe in God? Well then why don't you believe in me?"

That would have been an obvious question. "Of course," Jesus' disciples would have replied. Jesus was indicating that God is the source of everything and I am the same as God. To believe in God is to believe in Jesus as God.

Christ then is equally important as the object of your faith. You cannot isolate Christ Jesus from God. He was not merely a great prophet, as some religions believe. He is God.

In fact, Jesus states that the way his disciples manifested their faith in God was actually to believe in him. He was one with God in eternity past during the re-creation event (Gen. 1:26; John 1:1, 14:1). He also became the expression of God in human form to accomplish salvation (Matt. 1:21). Christ Jesus must be an object of your faith. Finally, Jesus says it is well pleasing to God that men direct their faith to him (John 6:29; Acts 20:21).

The Lord also makes an authoritative statement concerning the writings of Moses. He told the Jews that had they really given credence to Moses' writings, they would have believed Jesus was their promised Messiah (John 5:46, 47). If the Israelites really understood them, the Law would have stimulated their faith to receive their promised Messiah because contained in Moses' prose were words of prophecy concerning the Savior (Gen. 49:10; Deut. 18:15; Luke 16:31, 24:27; John 5:39).

The words of the prophets affect our faith as well. There is a story in the history of Israel concerning a man named Jehoshaphat (2 Chr. 20:1ff). He had enemies from Moab, Ammon and some of the Meunites who wanted to make war with him. After receiving this report, fear gripped Jehoshaphat's heart to such an extent that he proclaimed a fast and began to pray to God. While praying, the Spirit of God came upon an individual in the midst of them who began to prophesy words of victory. His prophetic words include the famous statement, *"...for the battle is not yours but God's"* (2 Chr. 20:15).

Jehoshaphat responds declaring, *"...put your trust in the LORD your God and you will be established. Put your trust in His prophets and succeed"* (2 Chr. 20:20).The prophetic words of Jahaziel became the focus point of Jehoshaphat's faith. The king believed they would see success on the battlefield because the words of the man of God.

The words of the prophets also affect the Church today (Luke 24:25). During one occasion, there was a plot to kill the apostle Paul (Acts 23:12). After soldiers moved him around attempting to avert his assassinated, he eventually appeared before the governor Felix to come face to face with his adversaries. His case was not resolved and would last for at least two more years (Acts 24:27). He then stood before Festus, who wanted to try him in Jerusalem, but Paul appealed to Caesar (Acts 25:10, 11). Finally, he stood before King Agrippa as he waited to see Caesar.

During his conversation with Agrippa, Paul began to talk about his past life when he persecuted the Christians. He also spoke about his subsequent conversion after which he began to witness for Christ. In concluding his defense, he asserts that the basis of his preaching comes from the writings of Moses and the Prophets (Acts 26:22). Next, he makes a very pointed question, *"King Agrippa, do you believe the Prophets?"*(Acts 26:27)

Unless we believe the writings of the Prophets, there is no basis for believing in Christ because the events of his life fulfilled many of their words. The writings of the Prophets must be an object of our faith. It was the weight of Paul's line of reasoning to the leaders, kings and to the Church (Eph. 2:20; 3:4-6). Throughout history, their words have been used to inspire faith in the hearts of God's people (Rom. 16:25, 26).

We are also told that our faith must be projected towards the gospel (Mark 1:14, 15). Besides defining it as the "good news," the gospel is the preaching of the coming kingdom of God which the Messiah will visibly establish in the future. The gospel must have an impact in our lives presently because it directly affects how we view the future. God gave us the gospel to inspire us today about life in the future.

When you placed your faith in the gospel, you acknowledged not only all that Christ has accomplished on your behalf, but that the Lord will be the spearhead of a future divine kingdom. Such acknowledgement of Christ as the Supreme Sovereign should usher in the "obedience of faith" (Rom. 16:26).

The objects of our faith help validate what we believe about God and why we believe it. Like road signs giving directions to a vehicle travelling on a highway, these objects keep us looking in the correct direction – towards God.

FOUR ASPECTS OF FAITH

Let's look at the four models of faith that are prominent in the Scriptures. These aspects of faith affect every believer. They are indispensable for furthering spiritual growth of the Body as well as being avenues by which God can work supernaturally in the lives of His people.

The Faith

This has nothing to do with what we expect or desire. "The faith" is a New Testament term referring to the system of belief that Christians adhere to. It encompasses the objective realities of what Christ has accomplished. In other words, it is the complete truth concerning all that Christ did and achieved on our behalf, along with the rules and regulations which govern the Christian life (Acts 16:7). There are several observations that I would like to make about the faith:

1. We must obey it. The objective truth must become a reality in your life (Acts 6:7; Rom. 1:5). God cannot do great and mighty things in your life if you are not obedient to the faith. The faith is the standard by which God regulates all His work. If you are not completely regulated by this system, you cannot receive God's best for your life.

2. You must persevere in the faith to have stability established in your soul and to maintain your focus on the purpose that Christ intended for your life. This, in turn will give you the confidence that you will be presented holy, without blemish and blameless when you stand before him (2 Tim. 4:7).

3. Your relationship with Christ is strengthened because you maintain your observance of the faith (Acts 16:5; 1 Cor. 16:13)

4. The standard of your life must be measured against the benchmark of the faith (2 Cor. 13:5). Success in life is not measure by how well you keep up with the Jones. It is determined by how much your life identifies with the Word of God.

5. The established goal for the Body of Christ is coming to the oneness of the faith (Eph. 4:13).

6. Faith and godly conduct maintain the reality of the faith your (1 Tim. 3:9).

7. Those who would teach false doctrine must be exposed and confronted with the faith in order that their teaching may become that which is free from any admixture of error (Titus 1:13).

8. You are to resist Satan based on the faith (1 Pet. 5:9).

9. It delivered us from bondage to the law (Gal. 3:23).

10. You must hold fast to the faith against any opposition (Jude 1:3).

The Gift of Faith

The gift of faith is a spiritual gift used for working miracles (1 Cor. 12:9). Not all believers possess this kind of faith. This is not the type of faith obtained because of believing in God daily. This is a unique gift, which God has given to some individuals to accomplish the most difficult tasks for the expressed purpose of serving and building up the Body of Christ (1 Cor. 12:7, 11).

If you look closely at verse eleven, you will notice that the Spirit invests these gifts into believers' lives. You can fast for 40 days, get up at 4:00 am every morning to pray for it or study all the scriptures you want, that will not get you this gift or any other in this chapter. The Holy Spirit only gives the gift of faith to believers "as He will".

The Fruit of Faith

As you look at Galatians 5:22, there is a reference to the "fruit of the Spirit" which manifests itself in nine ways. One of these is the fruit of faith. At first glance, it appears that this refers to your confidence in God to provide something you desire such as a car, job, home or spouse. However, upon close examination you will find that the emphasis is upon your character and not your faith itself (Matt. 25:21ff; John 15:8). Other translations such as the American Standard Version, Darby's Translation and the English Standard Version use the words fidelity or **faithfulness** instead of the word faith.

The emphasis of this word pertains to how much you can be relied upon to do what you are supposed to do. It speaks of a person who is trustworthy and faithful (1Cor. 4:2). This person will maintain the strictest commitment to lifestyle and service to the Lord at all cost (Luke 16:10, 11; Rev. 2:10).

This description of the fruit of faith can be substantiated by looking at Galatians chapter five. It is important to understand this aspect of faith as faithfulness because your success in the future judgement will depend on how faithful you are to Christ now. The criterion that Jesus Christ will use to determine if you will help him in the administration in his future kingdom is how faithful you were to him now. Do you actually think that Christ will allow you to rule over nations in his future visible kingdom for 1000 years, and you could not rule over your flesh for 60, 70 or 80 years now? Not faithful to him now – no ruling with him later.

Two particular sections of Scripture reveal special words of acknowledgment that Christ Jesus will declare to his servants. If you serve him exceptionally in this life, one particular statement you could hear is "Well done, good and **faithful** slave". You might even fit the qualification of a "**faithful** and sensible slave" (Matt. 25:21; Luke 12:42). Both of these words are from the same Greek word which means trustworthy. Being deemed faithful means that Christ was able to rely upon you to complete the business and commands he assigned to you.

Faith That Saves

This aspect of faith is limited to believing in Christ as our means of salvation. It is faith alone which God accepts as the basis by which He bestows upon us eternal life (Eph. 2:8). In God's New Testament economy, He used grace as a means of igniting our faith to believe Him for salvation. In regards to salvation, what are we to have faith in? We must believe that God raised Jesus from the dead (Rom. 10:9).

Placing our faith in Jesus' resurrection is imperative if we are going to believe in all that Christ accomplished through his Earthly life (1 Cor. 15:12-18). According to Paul, if we refuse to believe in Christ's resurrection, we have no security about our own resurrection.

We must also believe in the name of Christ (John 1:12, 3:18). This is significant. To believe in his name is to be reliant upon his character and divine authority. His power manifests through his name. Having faith in his name is equal to having faith in Jesus Christ himself (Acts 16:30, 31).

THE REALITY OF GOD'S EXISTENCE

As stated earlier, true faith encompasses the belief in the reality of God's existence. If God does not exist, then we have no reason for hope in an eternal future (Rom. 5:4, 5; 1 Cor. 13:13). Even though emphasis is placed on God as the source of all things, in reality, it was the complete Godhead which is accountable for creating all that exists (Gen. 1:1, 2, 26; Neh. 9:6; Col. 1:15-17). This is the substratum for believing everything else about God and His purposes.

As the writer of the Hebrews began to speak about faith, he made sure that he dealt with the reality of God's existence in his opening verses of chapter eleven, as this would become the reason why many of the patriarchs did what they did. He states, *"By faith we understand that the worlds were prepared by the word of God, so that what is seen was not made out of things which are visible"* (Heb. 11:3). This verse becomes the platform by which the writer introduces those who sought God's promises and obtained a favorable report from Him because of their lives.

Verse three holds the key to why Joshua believed that the walls of Jericho would fall. It is what motivated Joseph to speak to Israel about them leaving Egypt and to take his bones with them. It is why Moses was able to withstand Pharaoh until he released God's people from bondage.

These great men, as well as others in Hebrews chapter eleven, were able to believe God for the miraculous because they believed first and foremost in His existence.

The writer to the Hebrews indicates that the "things which are visible" gives us confidence about things which are "invisible". While faith is the "conviction of things **not seen**," the things that we see give us faith to believe in the unseen. Without visible evidence, we can't really believe that God exists. If you do not believe that God exists, how can you believe in His promises or anything else He declares about your life?

This is why the book of Romans explains it is important for you to be observant about God's creation. *"For since the creation of the world His invisible attributes, His eternal power and divine nature, have been clearly seen, being understood through what has been made..."* (Rom. 1:20).

Nature testifies of God's eternal power and character. People do not need a message preached to them about God. All they need to do is look around them. You can observe the green leaves on the trees, the soothing sound of the rain falling at 3:00 a.m., the depths of the oceans which do not overstep their boundaries to validate the existence of God.

If you look at life, understand that God created every natural thing you see, then nothing should hold you back from obtaining anything God has destined for your life. The only thing you need to do is continue learning about God and His attributes in order that your faith may continue to grow.

HE RULES ALL THINGS

Although important, faith in God's existence is not

sufficient. If this is all you believe, your faith is inadequate to change your life completely. Demons believe in God and tremble (James 2:19). Muslims believe God exists. Most people are looking to believe in a higher power. This is not the difficult process.

If you do not buy into the fact the God rules all things, then there is an issue. The reason why sometimes you lose consistency and stick-to-it-ness is because your faith allows you to believe in God's existence but does not provide enough force to believe that He can change your life. You have not conclusively decided within yourself that God rules all things.

This is why people get saved but the power of salvation does not manifest in its entirety. Most believers believe in God's existence, and see Jesus as the lamb who takes away all sin, but not as the ruler of their life. Only when God possesses absolute control over your life can He get some significant things accomplished. You will not be so quick to do or think what you want to. On the contrary, you will find out what He wants and base your life upon that premise.

If you recognize Him as ruler then no matter what happens in your life, you will know that God has the power to intervene (2 Chr. 29:11-13). You don't have to faint and stress out about issues that happen in your life. You do not have to worry about God taking care of you. You only need remain cool, calm and collected in the face of adversity because you realize that He rules everything.

You can also have confidence in His Word. If God rules all things, you can have faith to believe that whatever He says He will bring to pass (Acts 1:4-8; Heb. 1:2, 11:3). There is no one who can overrule God. His word is the final authority. When He speaks to you through His Word and by His Spirit, you can confidently move forward in that because there is no law higher than God's law. His sovereignty should render us obedient subjects. There is an old saying, "You can take that to the bank." This is precisely how you can feel about what God says concerning you. (Col. 3:24).

SALVATION THROUGH CHRIST

The final part of the definition of faith has to do with God providing salvation for us through Christ. Although God is the source, Christ became the channel (Eph. 2:1-8). Now we need to know what changes occurred when salvation took place. I am not presenting these events in any logical order. I am merely giving a capsule of what transpired.

There was a change in our spiritual position. God placed us into the sphere of Christ to guarantee our success while simultaneously introducing His Spirit into our lives (John 20:22; Rom. 6:3-5; Eph. 2:10). This securely united us to the benefits Christ gained on our behalf (Eph. 2:7).

This change in position parallels the fact that God brought us back into relationship with Himself. Once we are redeemed, the Bible applies to us the term "sons of God" or "children of God" which implies that we have been brought back into relationship with God (John 1:12; Rom. 8:14). The complete manifestation of what this means will be shown in the future when our bodies are redeemed from the Earth (Philip. 3:21; 1 Jn. 3:1, 2). The Bible calls this "adoption" (Rom. 8:19, 23).

Since we have become the sons of God, there are benefits we receive which includes our inheritance (Eph. 1:9-11; Col.

1:12, 3:24). The inheritance is "things" given to or entitled to us because we are sons (Luke 15:12, 13).

Inheritance has several applications that include: (A) property received such as land. This is what Israel was looking forward to (Deut. 4:38; Josh. 13:7) and (B) in the New Testament, it is the complete state of blessedness, which will be exemplified when Christ returns to establish his kingdom. This state of blessedness is not only salvation, but the **benefits or rewards** to be enjoyed because of salvation (Rom. 8:17). This inheritance can be lost (1 Cor. 6:9; Gal. 5:21; Eph. 5:5).

HOW FAITH IS STIMULATED

There are at least five avenues that God uses to stimulate faith to believe Him for recovery. One of the greatest ways God uses to inspire faith is His Word (Rom. 10:17). However, the only way to produce faith in our heart is if we allow ourselves to believe that what we hear is truth. When you hear the gospel, if you have a closed heart and mind, there will be no manifestation of faith. You have to allow the Word to become the primer of our faith.

In conjunction with the Word is the aspect of preaching. After all, how can people hear the gospel without God sending a preacher of righteousness (Rom. 10:14)? The great wisdom of God is to use the method of spoken words to capture the minds of hearers (1 Cor. 1:18, 21, 25). It is imperative that you do not neglect your responsibility as a believer to share your faith whenever possible. There may be people who do not believe because you have not spoken.

Another way which God uses to produce faith is miracles. In the gospel of John, there was a prominent man whose son was at the point of death. The man heard that Jesus was close by and went to meet him, requesting that his son be healed. In response to his request, Jesus says, *"Unless you people see signs and wonders, you simply will not believe"* (John 4:46-48). The fact remains, some people will not believe in Jesus until they see a supernatural event occur.

The people who stood by watching Jesus hanging on the cross were such individuals. As they hurled taunting insults at him, some of them said, *"... let Him now come down from the cross, and we will believe in Him"* (Matt. 27:42). Sometimes it just takes God working in a supernatural way for people who believe in Him.

God also works miracles through the lives of His servants in order that people may believe in Him (Ex. 10:1, 2; Mark 16:17, 18; Acts 2:1ff, 3:1ff; 1 Cor. 2:4, 5). Just as God worked miracles in the Bible, I believe that miracles are for today. Certain environments that we enter, God must show that He is alive through healing the sick, opening blind eyes etc.

God also uses words of prophecy to activate faith in an individual's heart (1 Sam. 22:15; 2 Sam. 2:10-15; Ezra 5:1, 2). When Paul wrote his letter to the believers at Corinth, he stated that prophecy was for the purpose of "edification and exhortation and consolation" (1 Cor. 14:3).

According to the apostle Paul, the two groups of people who are affected by prophesying are "unbelievers" and those who are "ungifted" which refers to Christians (1 Cor. 14:24). The result of prophesying will be to convict them of unbelief, error or sin (1 Cor. 14:31). It is only through this type of prophesying that men's secrets are revealed causing them to worship God which is definitely an act prompted by faith (1 Cor. 14:25).

Without faith operating in your life, you will not be completely motivated to pursue the great things, which God has in store for you. After all, the greatest blessings are things "which are invisible".

THE DOCTRINE OF BAPTISMS

Although the theme of baptism reverberates throughout the New Testament pages, it has its roots in the traditions of the Old Testament. This act of baptism pervaded Jewish society. However, the converts in the book of Hebrews needed to understand it in terms of the doctrine of Christ. Barring the new birth experience, baptism is perhaps one of the most significant events that can happen in a believer's life. Thus, the writer of Hebrew included the "doctrine of baptisms" (Heb. 6:2).

From the opening words contained in the Recreation account to the Flood of Noah, we see that God intends to use water and the Spirit to effect change in peoples' lives and circumstances. Because baptism is such a vital experience in the life of a believer, we must understand what the Bible says about it.

Simplistically, baptism is for the purpose of identification with a person, process or a group of people. It takes on varying degrees to accomplish God's total purpose of identification and purification. As you study this section, you will see that baptism will distinguish one group of people from another such as the baptism of fire and the baptism into the body of Christ. Everyone will be affected by baptism sooner or later. If you are not a participant in the baptism experiences now as a believer, the only one left for you to experience is the baptism of fire in the future.

There are eleven significant baptisms in the Bible. Out of

these eleven, only six have anything to do with water; yet, when people discuss the subject of baptism, many equate it strictly with water. Preachers have taught their constituents for centuries, principally about water baptism. As a result, this has become primarily one of few that believers are knowledgeable about. The other well-known baptism is that of the Holy Ghost. However, there are others which are significant to our understanding of what God is attempting to do through baptism. If you do not get a grasp of all 11, you will not have a comprehensive perspective of God's total intention through the act of baptism.

When attempting to understand the process of baptism, you cannot start from the New Testament. Doing this is like trying to understand a movie by starting with the climax first. Although you may understand to a small degree what the movie was about, you cannot fully ascertain all the details of the movie. If you are reading a good mystery novel, you do not start with finding out who committed the crime, you start with the facts of the crime and read through the investigation. Only then can you understand how the criminals were apprehended. It is the same with baptism. You must understand the significance of baptism in the Old Testament before you can appreciate it's outworking in the New Testament. If you cannot understand how God worked in the lives of people who lived before you, it will be difficult for you to identify His move in the present.

Some of the baptisms which occurred in the Old Testament do not affect us today. They stricly historical. However, the apostle Paul said we should not be ignorant of them because they became symbolic for what God intends to do in our life presently. Therefore, we must begin with looking at baptism from the Old Testament.

The Jews were accustomed to what was termed washings or purification. These washing were types of baptisms. Washings or purifications were a daily practice for God's people as prescribe by their great leader Moses (Lev. 12, 14:7). These cleanings foreshadowed the process that water would play in the separation of believers from uncleanness and the world. It would also hint at individual's future identification with the work of Christ.

Ritual immersion provided cleansing for the priests, which allowed them to enter pure and sacred areas in the Temple. This also enabled them to participate in other sacred events. In fact, without participating in these washings, no Israelite would have been able to function properly in the Jewish society. Even for those who would become converts, the primary way for them to identify with Judaism was through baptism (Acts 10:46-48).

Although these washings were a part of the daily life of the Jews, the writer to the Hebrews intended to show that these were symbols and pointed to God's work in the New Testament. The author knew that without baptism, a Jew's religious activity was incomplete; therefore, he had to address the issue of baptism in the book of Hebrews.

As we study baptism from both the Old and New Covenants, you will begin to understand that this act was to find its meaning and fulfillment in the work of Christ. Although baptism has become a symbol for a person's death to sin, their cleansing from it and their new life in Christ, it would also become one of the most profound and prolific works of the Holy Spirit in the life of a believer to empower them for service (Acts 2:41; Rom. 6:4; Eph. 5:26).

The eleven baptisms includes: the baptism of Noah and Moses (symbolic), the baptism of John and Jesus (transitional), the baptisms of the Holy Ghost, fire, into the body of Christ, suffering, the Word, for the dead (present and future experiences) and other washings (ceremonial).

BAPTISM DEFINED

There are several definitions of the word we translate baptism. The first Greek word is *bapto* which means "to dip, to whelm, and to cover wholly with fluid" (John 13:26; Luke 16:24). All other definitions are expansions of this word.

Second, the word *baptisma* means baptism, consisting of the process of immersion (Matt. 3:11; Acts 19:3; Rom. 6:4; 1 Cor. 12:13; Eph. 4:5).

The third is *baptizo*. This definition means to baptize, immerse, sink, bathe, wash, and dip in or under. This word primarily refers to the baptism of John and Christians in reference to ritualistic practices (Mark 1:4; John 3:22, 23; Acts 2:41; 1 Cor. 1:17).

The fourth word is *Baptismos*is. This is the verb form of bapto and refers to the act of baptizing. It means to immerse. This word also concerns ceremonial washings (Mark 7:4; Heb. 9:10).

There is one another significant word in the New Testament that refers to baptism. The word *loutron* or "washing" means to bathe. It is figurative of baptism and washing. *Loutron* comes from the Greek word *louo*, which means, "to bathe the whole person". The purpose for this washing is for cleansing. We will discuss this in depth when we discuss the baptism of the Word.[1]

THE METHOD OF BAPTISM

From the definitions provided, it seems that the logical method of baptism would to immerse an individual in water. This represents that the total person is dealt with. Without using the method of immersion, it would be difficult understand some important scriptures such as (Mark 1:10).

Consider this, the Bible states that John was baptizing *"in Aenon near Salim, because there was much water there..."* (John 3:23). If John were only sprinkling, there would be no need to mention that he baptized in that location because there was an abundance of water.

The epistle to the Colossians also supports immersion. It states that we were *"buried with Him in baptism."* Subsequently, we were *"raised up with Him"* (Col. 2:12). Burial symbolizes going down to the grave while rising symbolizes coming up out of it.

In further support of immersion, text concerning the baptism process by the Essenes says that the place used to baptize had to contain no less than 150-200 gallons of water. Why would there be conditions set as to the amount of water if one was only going to sprinkle?

The Seventh-day Adventists have found paintings and carvings in catacombs and churches supporting baptism by immersion. Other places around the world such as North Africa, Italy and France have pieces of antiquity that also supports this perspective.

As you begin to read other materials, you will begin to see that there are overwhelming facts that the normal mode of baptism in the early church was immersion.

Many disagree with the process of immersion. However, the procedure of baptism must not become a point of contention between believers. The main point is that baptism is a pivotal experience in the lives of individuals (believers and unbelievers).

TYPES OF BAPTISMS

The Baptism of Noah

There is a familiar story in the Scripture that many of us learned at an early age while attending Sunday school, a Christian School or Vacation Bible School. It was the story of Noah and his ark (Gen. 6-8).

I can remember being astonished that water covered the entire world. It was difficult to fathom that God rained so much water that nothing of the Earth remained uncovered. As I began to grow spiritually, I began to see that this act represented many things, among them baptism. Let us rehearse the story of Noah.

During this time, humanity's wickedness grew to know no bounds. Although we do not have the complete details of that society's debauchery, we have a glimpse of the deeds that aroused God's anger and judgement.

In Genesis chapter six, as a prelude to the flood, some of the angels looked upon the beauty of the human women and wanted to have sex with them. They decided to materialize in human form (flesh) without God's permission. They married these women, had sexual relations with them with the result of bearing children called Nephilim. The union of the angels with the humans created an offspring that God never intended to dwell upon the Earth.

The offspring of these individuals were extremely tall, strong, intelligent, and began to conquer the entire Earth. Since they would also have elongated life spans, God had to fix their years to no more than one hundred and twenty (Gen. 6:1-11).

God became grieved because of the moral decadence in His creation. He decided to destroy humankind completely with the exception of Noah and his family. Subsequently, God commissions Noah to build an ark. In essence, God saved and separated Noah from the evil of society through water. Why did God save Noah? According to the Scripture, he was righteous (Gen. 6:9, 7:1). He walked with God continually.

The salvation of Noah through a flood became a type for us representing the baptism of the believer. Just as the water was a distinguishing mark for Noah, physically separating him from the evil of his generation, so water baptism would become a sign that a believer is now separated from the world and therefore no longer subject to the impending wrath of God (1 Thes. 1:10, 5:9).

Peter writes concerning baptism as it relates to Noah. In his first epistle chapter three, we find the apostle dealing with Christian conduct (evil conduct was the cause of the flood). He addresses issues such as compassion, unity, brotherly love, evil speaking, suffering and having a good conscience (1 Pet. 3:8-18). It is within this context that the following passage concerning the baptism of Noah and his family appears:

"In which also He went and made proclamation to the spirits now in prison, who once were disobedient, when the patience of God kept waiting in the days of Noah, during the construction of the ark, in which a few, that is, eight persons, were brought safely

through the water. Corresponding to that, baptism now saves you—not removal of dirt from the flesh, but an appeal to God for a good conscience—through the resurrection of Jesus Christ..." (1 Pet. 3:19-21).

The flood which delivered Noah and his household from the former life of sin, typified through the wickedness of his generation, into a new life and environment was a picture of what happens for you and I upon baptism. If the baptism of the believers is the representation of this event, then it also typifies our deliverance from the former state of sin into a new one through the resurrection of Christ Jesus (Rom. 6:1ff).

In First Peter, we see three elements: Christ (vs. 18), Noah (vs. 20) and baptism (vs. 21). Just as the ark became the vessel to bring safety and salvation to Noah and his family, Christ was the vessel God used to bring safety and salvation to those who would believe in him.

Those who had the gospel preached to them by Noah and yet withheld their faith from participating in his beliefs (this is the meaning of disobedient) were preached to by Christ during his three days of sojourning beneath the Earth (vs. 18).

Peter brings the disobedient into context here because they did not have a peaceful conscience with God. This is the aim of the passage (vs. 16). In light of the fact that Noah had a "good conscience," God, spared him from the judgement of the world through the deluge.

Notice, what saved him was that his conscience was at peace with God. In the terms of that dispensation, he had salvation before his separation through water. His experience of water did not cause him to be in right relationship with God. He was already at peace with God (Gen. 6:9, Heb. 11:7).

Peter thus uses the episode of Noah to show us the effects that the baptism has upon believers. This baptism distinguishes those who have believed into Christ (the obedient - Noah, believers) from those who refuse (the disobedient - people in Noah's day, unbelievers). Peter assures us that baptism requests of God that we have a pure (good) conscience before Him.

He uses the word "appeal" in connection with a good conscience (1 Pet. 3:21). The word indicates a request or earnest seeking. Understanding that makes this passage somewhat clearer.

Baptism itself does not deliver you from the filth of the flesh but is symbolic of your request to God to deliver you from a defiled conscience. Baptism delivers you from a guilty conscience and shows that you have peace with God by identifying with the death burial and resurrection of Jesus Christ (Heb. 10:22). Although Noah's baptism was a physical separation from the depravity of the world, baptism for us shows our separation internally because of what God has done in our conscience.

The Baptism into Moses

Another Important baptism occurred when Israel passed through the Red Sea (1 Cor. 10:1, 2). Moses, as the servant of God, delivered Israel from Egypt by the power of God. Their captivity in Egypt was the greatest time of bondage they had ever known (Ex. 1:8-11). It would last approximately four hundred years according to the time mentioned to Abraham by God (Gen. 15:13; Ex. 12:40).

When the time of their release had come, Moses instructed each family to sacrifice a lamb, applying its blood to the two side posts and the upper post of the house (Ex. 12:1ff). That night God performed His last miracle in the process of Israel's deliverance from Egypt. All the firstborn of Egypt were slew (Ex. 11:1-6). The devastation of this phenomenon forced Pharaoh to release the Israelites from their captivity.

After the Hebrews departed from Egypt, Pharaoh considered what happened. Possibly, he thought Moses used some magical spell on him. Coming to his senses, Pharaoh figured he should have never allowed his Hebrew slaves to leave Egypt. He felt the immediate impact of not having any servants to build his cities; therefore, he pursued the Israelites to recapture them (Ex. 14:5).

Ramses II marshalled his army of six hundred chariots, fifty thousand equestrians and two hundred thousand footmen. They began their pursuit about thirty days after the Israelites had departed. Eventually, Pharaoh and his army found them in a narrow place with a ridge of mountains against the Israelites on both sides so that there was no way of escape except thru the Red Sea. Pharaoh believed he had the advantage, concluding that the Israelites were weary due to their journey in the desert; consequently, it would be easy to overtake them and bring them back to Egypt. This brings us to the conclusion of one of the most celebrated of all stories in the Bible, the crossing of the Red Sea.

As the Israelites saw the Egyptians approaching with their mighty army, suddenly, a horror they had never known pierced their hearts. The Hebrews believed they were about to breathe their last breath. In their fear, they cried unto Moses that he should have left them alone in Egypt to remain servants, not understanding that the situation which caused their greatest fear would consequently bring them their greatest joy. God was about to rid the Israelites of their captors.

In response to a command from God, Moses lifted up his rod, stretched his hand out over the sea and commanded it to separate (Ex. 14:16). A strong east wind blew all night over the Red Sea. This episode ended with approximately two million people with their beasts crossing through the sea on dry ground. As the Egyptians pursued, they would see the wall of waters return upon their army causing their deaths by drowning.

Paul reminds us of this episode in First Corinthians. In chapter 10, the apostle Paul uses this event to instruct the believers at Corinth. He does not want the Red Sea episode to be absent from their remembrance. Paul writes that everything recorded about Israel's experiences "...were our examples..." (1 Cor. 10:13).

According to the apostle, the act of Israel passing through the Red Sea represented baptism. *"For I do not want you to be unaware, brethren, that our fathers were all under the cloud and all passed through the sea; and all were baptized into Moses in the cloud and in the sea..."* (1 Cor. 10:1-2).

There are three primary elements here: the cloud, the sea and Moses. The cloud represents the Holy Spirit which leads believers on their journey (Ex. 13:21, 22). It is the Spirit that led them to the point of emersion into water by Moses (Ex. 13:21, 22, 14:19).

Moses is a type of Christ. God delivered the Israelites from their bondage through the sphere of Moses. Just as the

Israelites were baptized into Moses, we are baptized into Jesus Christ (Rom. 6:3-5; Gal. 3:27).

Then there was the Red Sea. God used water to deliver Noah and again used water to deliver the Hebrews from Egypt. The baptism into Moses eradicated the old life that Israel knew. They were beginning a new spiritual journey into the divine covenant of God with Moses through baptism. The Red Sea event was not just the separating of one group of people from another. It was their initiation into the covenant promises.

This is extremely important. God reigns on the just as well as the unjust; however, there are certain things that He will not do for people unless they have been united to Christ. He is only obligated to those who are a part of the covenant blessings of Christ. People forfeit the greatest blessing they could have because they are not rightly connected to the sphere through which the most comprehensive blessings flow.

Notice, they were baptized into Moses; however, most of them died in the wilderness because God was not pleased with their lives. Take this with a grain of salt, but many of the saints God is not pleased with. This is what Paul shows us in First Corinthians.

The apostle used this episode in the same manner that Peter used the incident of the flood. These apostles wanted to show their perspective audiences that these events point to what Christ did for us. God used baptism to show our union with Christ. It is through baptism into his death and body that we are bound to him (Eph. 4:5).

What must be noted in First Corinthians is the word "moreover" in the King James Version (1 Cor. 10:1). This word ties the act of the Red Sea to the discourse about Christian living which Paul attaches to contending in sporting competitions (1 Cor. 6:1-9:27). The goal of the competition is to win the prize, avoiding disqualification from the race. The prize for you and I is Christ and his kingdom (Philip. 3:8, 12).

Although the Israelites were initiated into this Mosaic covenant through baptism, many of them were disqualified from Canaan (type of the kingdom) because of their lusts and unbelief (Num. 14:20-23, 29, 30; 1 Cor. 10:5, 8). Paul notes that it takes disciplining one's life to qualify for the prize – the kingdom (1 Cor. 9:24-27).

The apostle intended for the first portion of chapter ten to remind us that God made provisions and privileges for his people; however, many failed to enjoy the benefits of the covenant via baptism into Moses.

Our baptism into Christ's death and body is an awe-inspiring event in our lives. It is one of God's ways of helping us become partakers of privileges that He has prepared for us. Nevertheless, if we fail to discipline our lives, then you and I will find ourselves coming up short as many of the Israelites did in the wilderness. May we all bring into the realm of our experience the complete work of Christ.

The Baptism of John

John's baptism of repentance was transitional, used strictly to prepare individuals for the coming Messiah and his reign (Matt. 3:1ff; Acts 19:4). His message and ministry was unique and dealt with a specific group of people for a specific time. It does not apply to any person who believed in the Jesus after his ascension.

We must not say that his ministry abrogated the Law of Moses; it enabled people to position themselves to abide by the Law because of Christ. John's baptism became a transitional point between the some of the rituals of the Old Testament the New (Matt. 11:13; Luke 16:16; Acts 1:21, 22).

A divine era was beginning where people could live under the enabling influence of grace (Rom. 6:14; Gal. 1:6). As God unites us to Christ, the power of his life within us (which is the power of grace) works for us in a way that the Law never could (Rom. 8:1-4). This is what repentance was all about for those exposed to John's preaching.

The reason why the apostle Paul referred to John's baptism as one of repentance is because his baptism was symbolic of people's repentance (Mark 1:4). It was through baptism that people exemplified their repentance and their belief in the coming Messiah. It was as if John used water as a symbolic pledge of repentance. In fact, the definition of "baptism of repentance" indicates that everyone who participated in this event was bound to repentance. God considered this to be the seal of their confession.

Repentance though was only a part of what John's baptism was to accomplish. The other aspect is that these same individuals became qualified to partake of the benefits in the future kingdom of Christ. This is extremely important to remember.

The baptism of repentance was about repositioning people to operate under the new dispensational economy that God was to establish through Christ (John. 1:17). This is why John's message was *"Repent, **for the kingdom of heaven is at hand"** (Matt. 3:2). Jesus, his disciples and the apostles preached this message (Matt. 4:17, 10:7, 24:14).

The Law given to Moses was the initiation of how God desired humanity to operate to be pleasing to Him, but the future kingdom would express the perfect order of things. God gathers everyone who believes in Christ into the kingdom, establishing a society of people intimately united to Him (Eph. 2:19). Thus, as citizens of the divine kingdom, we have the opportunity to enjoy all the benefits of salvation that Christ has gained and God has purposed for us. In short, the baptism of repentance was symbolic of one's turning from the Law of Moses toward the kingdom of heaven – God's New Testament economy.

There are two groups of people we must consider as we observe John's baptism. The first is those who would believe and repent submitting to John's message. Secondly, there were the scoffers, the religious leaders of the day which included the Pharisees and Sadducees (Matt. 3:5ff; Luke 7:29, 30).

The first group of individuals were comprised of the Jews in general, the publicans (Jewish tax collectors) and the soldiers (we cannot be sure if these were Jewish or Roman) (Matt. 3:5, 6; Luke 3:10-14). This shows the amazing impact that John's ministry and message had on the public. Individuals who had hatred for one another were gathered together, reasoning among themselves about who John actually was.

He was the last prophet before the appearance of Christ. Jews knew that prophets spoke the words of God and represented His authority. John taught many things in such a way as to invoke the anticipation of the people for this kingdom (Luke 3:15, 18). He baptized those who believed with water. These are the also the group of people who would be baptized with the Holy Ghost (Matt. 3:11; Acts 1:8).

The second group of people consisted of the majority of the Pharisees, Sadducees and others who refused to believe John's message. John called these two groups of religious leaders a "generation of vipers" (Luke 3:7). This statement speaks of their wickedness.

John's baptism was an enormous problem for those religious leaders. As staunch constituents of the Law of Moses, they rejected any teaching not conducive for the way of living that they were accustomed; and John's message violated many of their beliefs and customs.

The first thing John did was to break away from the traditions of sacrifice for sins. To deal with sins under the Mosaic covenant, they sacrificed animals, shedding their blood. However, John used water as a means of dealing with sins. This was a serious blow to their system.

In addition, sacrificing animals to deal with sin was a job that pertained to the priests alone (Ex. 29; Lev. 1:6ff, 4:1ff). The Sadducees and Pharisees would not submit and repent to anyone except the priest. Even though he was not a priest, John still brought them face-to-face with their sin, making it personal, but they refused to believe his message.

To illustrate how offensive John was to these religious leaders, we can look at church society today. What John did was the equivalent of a general member in the church going to a Bishop and telling them that they needed to repent for his sins when the Bishop believed he had already dealt with his sins. They would look at that person and want to say, "Will you get out of my face." "Who do you think you are?" This is exactly what is happening with John.

In a beautiful play on their system of sacrifice, John the Baptist tells them to *"Bear fruit in keeping with repentance"*

(Matt. 3:8). Sacrificing animals was a way they visibly showed their repentance under the regulations given by Moses. John did not release them from providing visible proof that they wanted what he was offering – the kingdom (Lev. 4:22-24). They needed to show John they were serious about what he had to offer. The only way for those religious leaders to do that was to bring him visible proof which they would not.

These spiritual champions of the Law also had a problem with the act of the baptism itself. If they stepped into the river, they were admitting that their religious system was done away with and they were indeed sinners. This, they would never do. They were well aware of the reasons for why they needed to wash. It was either for the priest to come into God's presence (Ex. 30:18-21; 2 Chr. 4:2, 6) or if they were defiled in some way (Num. 19).

These "spiritual ones" prided themselves on upholding the Law in the strictest sense, so to them, there was no need to be baptized by John. In their mind, they thought they were already holy because they were the descendants of Abraham (Luke 3:8). Instead, the Pharisees and Sadducees thought they would participate in the kingdom because of their lineage. However, participation in the coming kingdom was to be by faith and not because of their ancestry.

John, a man with a radical message, confronted the religious leaders as well as all others about their sin in order for them to participate in the coming kingdom of Christ. For us, the kingdom is not something merely in the future. We are operating in it presently, will participate in it in the future, and instead of water, we are brought into the kingdom through the operation of the Holy Spirit and faith (John 3:3, 5; Titus 3:5-7).

The Baptism of Jesus

Since Christ was without sin in his humanity, his baptism must have been different from the others, even though it occurred within the context of John's baptism (Heb. 4:15; 1 Pet. 3:21, 22). The Bible explicitly states what Jesus' baptism was all about. In his own words, Jesus tells John that he should be baptized to "fulfill all righteousness" (Matt. 3:15). The vast majority of theologians agree that his baptism has a multiplicity of meanings:

A. Jesus' baptism was preparation for his ministry. Every priest consecrated to minister unto God, standing as a representative for the people washed with water. Thus, this baptism was Jesus' initiation into the priesthood.

B. As a lamb, he became our sacrifice. Therefore, he needed washing. In the Old Testament, the parts of the sacrifice were to be washed before they were placed on the altar (Ex. 29:17; Lev. 1:9-13; John 1:29). His baptism meant that he was eligible to die.

C. Jesus' baptism was a way for him to identify with humanity. Everyone will go through a baptism at some point in time.

D. It identified him as the Son of God (Luke 3:21, 22; John. 1:29-34). This was God's way of giving accreditation to Jesus' life and ministry (1 Jn. 5:8, 9).

E. His baptism symbolized the total dedication of Christ in fulfilling God's complete plan to save all that would believe in him (Mark 1:11; Luke 3:22).

F. This visually showed the process of Jesus' death, burial and resurrection.[2]

There are numerous other reasons as to what the

significance of Jesus' baptism was. The main point is that Jesus' baptism showed his continuation in the process of "fulfillling all righteousness".

The Baptism of the Holy Spirit

During John's recorded message, he introduces the coming Messiah by declaring that the coming Messiah's strength surpassed that of his own (Matt. 3:11). Christ is stronger both to save and to punish. It is Christ's ministry that would cause a new beginning for some and the tormenting end for others.

Upon believing in John's message, those baptized were also promised the baptism of the Holy Ghost. This is also affectionately known as the outpouring of the Holy Spirit (Isa. 44:3, 4; Joel 2:28, 29; Acts 1:4-8, 2:17, 18). This baptism is so essential, that without it, you cannot fully participate in the kingdom of God. Without this baptism, it is **impossible** to experience the fullness of life as God intended.

This baptism of the Spirit has an inward and outward working in our lives. The inward aspect of baptism deals with the changing and purifying of our soul, which cannot be accomplished apart from being united with Christ (1 Cor. 6:17). God accomplishes this by baptizing us into Christ or his body.

When a person is baptized in the Holy Spirit, they are immersed in the influences of the Spirit which empowers them for service (John. 14:26, Acts 1:8). Thus, the baptism of the Holy Ghost brings change to you internally before God uses you externally.

The baptism of the Holy Spirit is promised in connection with the preaching of the kingdom. Therefore, this baptism is primarily for equipping believers to operate in it. You will never be completely equipped and empowered to serve the Lord in kingdom unless you have experienced this baptism.

This baptism of the Holy Spirit could not take place until Jesus Christ ascended (John 16:7). After his ascension, the apostles became the first recipients (John 20:22). Later, other disciples received the Holy Ghost by placing their faith in Christ (Acts 2:38, 19:5, 6; Gal. 3:2).

It is also through this baptism of the Spirit that we experience the blessings of the divine life in Christ. As we participate in His kingdom, God releases everything we need through the agency of the Holy Spirit (Prov. 1:23; Joel 2:28, 29). The connection of God's kingdom and the Holy Spirit is so important that Jesus delayed his ascension into heaven until he communicated to his disciples everything he wanted them to know about the kingdom (Acts 1:3).

Any significant impact that you will have in the kingdom only happens after you receive this baptism. After Jesus concluded his teaching series, he ascended, and this baptism occurred sometime later. Notice, the baptism of the Spirit only occurred after they had sufficient knowledge about the kingdom of God.

External Signs of Spirit Baptism

There are various indicators that you have received the baptism of the Holy Spirit. It is unfortunate that some people have limited the experience of this baptism to speaking in tongues. Speaking in tongues is only an expression. As we carefully read the scriptures we will see that as Christ pours out the Spirit upon mankind, there are other visible aspects of this baptism (Acts 2:17,18).

If you do not understand all the signs of this baptism, you will limit yourself from experiencing all that God wants to do when this baptism occurs because emphasis has been placed on **an** evidence, not **the** evidence. **An** evidence is tongues, prophecy or dreams. **The** evidence is power. Is there no wonder why the work of God has been limited? Let's discuss some of these signs.

One expression is prophecy (Acts 2:17). Prophecy here is often misunderstood. This is not prophecy in general. It is one who speaks under Divine inspiration things that pertain especially to the kingdom of God. Believers with this expression speak about what God wants to do in His kingdom more so than in an individual's life. It is prophecy about the kingdom agenda.

Another expression is visions. Notice in Acts chapter two that the "young men" shall see "visions". The definition of "young men" implies that this person is less than 40 years old. I believe the reason is contained within the words "see visions". It takes time and energy to see visions. There is an extremely intense feeling and action that accompanies visions.

In particular, visions here means that the work of the Holy Spirit will reveal Christ as the Messiah in such an intense way that it will prompt one into action (Acts 10:9ff). Visions usually happen while the individual is awake (Acts 2:17).

Dreams, on the other hand, usually occur when the individual is asleep. They do not necessarily prompt people to work. The Bible states that old men will "dream dreams" when the baptism of the Holy Spirit is experienced.

The designations of sons, daughters, elders and

handmaidens (women slaves) merely imply that Christ will baptize all humanity without respect of persons. As indication of this, John baptized men and women both old and young (Mark 1:4, 5).

Signs and wonders will also be evident. Signs are remarkable occurrences that transcend the normal course of nature. Wonders usually pertain to performing miracles. Although Peter uses these words in reference to the change in the natural course of events in the future, this was yet to be an active way of the Spirit manifesting himself in the lives of people (Mark 16:17, 20; John 4:48, 20:30; Acts 2:43, 14:1-3).

Perhaps one of the greatest aspects of these signs and wonders is the Earth will undergo cataclysmic changes (Acts 2:19, 20). In preparation for the return of the Lord, God promised that "signs and wonders" would be demonstrated **upon** the Earth. It seems that the Scripture is indicating the Earth would also be a recipient of the work of the Holy Spirit. If this is the case it is neither something new nor the last time it will happen. During the recreation event, the Earth was a recipient of the work of the Holy Spirit (Gen. 1:2). At the conclusion of the age, the Earth will undergo another renovation process (Isa. 65:17; 2 Pet. 3:12, 13; Rev. 21:1).

An additional manifestation of the one receiving the outpouring of the Holy Spirit is speaking in tongues (Acts 2:4). This is what many people use to identify the Holy Spirit baptizism, but there are two types of tongues: the tongues of men and unknown tongues.

Speaking in the tongues of men means that people are able to talk in a foreign language without having any type of training. For instance, let's say you are a citizen of the

United States, but God begins to move on you and you begin speaking fluent Spanish to Spaniards without ever taking a formal class or studying Rosetta Stone. This would be a supernatural occurrence. This is exactly what happened on the day of Pentecost. People began to speak in other native languages without any type of training. To those standing around listening, this was bizarre.

The reason why God allowed this to happen is because there were so many people of other nationalities present at the outpouring of the Holy Spirit. This became a great and effective witness for the Christians (Acts 2:1-12). From this experience, Peter was able to preach a message that would persuade thousands to believe in Christ (Acts 2:40, 41).

An unknown tongue is a spiritual language people use when speaking to God. Our natural mind cannot understand this language. Just as the Spirit works to speak this language through an individual, He must inspire either you or another person to interpret what is said (1 Cor. 14:2).

Christ's purpose for giving his power to the Church through his Spirit is for the purpose of them becoming individuals who can give powerful demonstration to who he is. Ultimately, the baptism of the Holy Spirit is the power of the Spirit coming upon you and I for effective service in the kingdom (Acts 1:8).

The greatest way to examine if you have been baptized is by examining your witness. If there are no other apparent signs of this baptism, you should examine if your life exhibits the power of God causing you to have significant impact others around you.

Finally, if you want to know how to receive the baptism of the Holy Spirit there is one answer that becomes the summation for all others. According to the book of Acts, the Holy Spirit is given to those who obey the instruction concerning Christ (John 7:38, 39; Acts 5:32). If you are living a life of obedience to Christ, ask him to baptize you in the Holy Ghost. He will honor your request.

The Baptism of Fire

Whereas the baptism of the Holy Spirit is for our present experience, the baptism of fire pertains strictly to the future. We have pondered the fact that there were two groups of people at John's baptism. There were also two baptisms that he mentioned. Christ would baptize believers with the Holy Ghost while reserving the most terrifying judgement for unbelievers – the baptism of fire (Luke 3:16). There are several perspectives concerning this "baptism of fire".

Some suppose that God uses this baptism as a way to rid sin out of a person's life. The ultimate goal of this baptism, they believe, is to usher one into holiness. They use First Corinthians 3:12-16 to validate their point. However, I disagree with this perspective. To interpret the passage in First Corinthians as the baptism of fire would do much harm to that passage. While I agree that the judgement of the believers will be through fire, it is for the purpose of examination not purification. Neither is it a baptism. It is strictly a time of judgement for believers.

Another point of conflict is this judgement by fire takes place during "the day" (1 Cor. 3:13). "The day" refers to Christ's return from heaven. He will raise the dead and execute his final judgement before establishing his kingdom. Consequently, there will be no time for this fire to purify anyone bringing about an increased state of holiness. The only thing I do agree with is that the baptism of fire will take place during Christ's Second Advent.

Others believe that this baptism accompanies that of the Holy Ghost in empowering a person for service (Acts 2:1-4). There is still a problem with this perception. The baptism of believers in Acts was a positive one whereas the baptism of fire encountered in Luke has a negative impact.

A final point of view is that this "baptism of fire" is for non-believers. As you examine Luke chapter three you will see a clear distinction between the two groups of people. The wheat (believers) will be gathered into the barn for safekeeping while the chaff (non-believers) will experience a fire that no water can quench (Matt. 3:12; Luke 3:17).

This baptism of fire literally refers to the fire of hell. It speaks of the extreme penalty of sin, which is the culmination of the "wrath to come" (Luke 3:7). This wrath of God brings all the penalties that unbelievers will secure for themselves at the last day (1 Thes. 1:10, 2:16

John uses the word fire three times in Luke chapter three. In verse 10, the unfruitful trees are "cast into the fire". Verse 11 says that those who do not believe will be "baptized in fire". Finally, verse 12 says that this is an "unquenchable fire". This final judgement of fire will occur when the eye of the unbeliever has closed in this life and God raises them to stand at the great white throne (Matt. 25:41, 46; John 15:5, 6; Rev. 20:14).

The reason why the Bible defines this experience as a baptism is because the place where these individuals will be cast is called a "lake of fire". Just as John immersed others in water with Jesus subsequently baptizing them in the Holy Spirit, similarly, there will be an immersion for unbelievers in fire (20:15).

Whether this will be an actual lake is questionable by some. For them, this merely speaks of extreme punishment in the future. Whatever you believe, just know that the extreme torment, pain and anguish that will come as a result of this punishment is so unfathomable that Jesus himself came, died and rose again to appease God's judgement of sin in order that you would not have to experience this baptism of fire. Those who find this as their experience will be forever condemned there.

Another important fact of this baptism is that brimstone fuels this fire (Rev. 21:8). Brimstone is used as a perpetual fuel for the fire ensuring that it will never go out (Gen 19:24; Ps. 11:6; Ezek. 38:22). Therefore, the baptism of fire is an eternal judgement.

Baptism into the Body of Christ

This baptism is significant because it unites believers to each other and Christ. This is the only thing that rescues us from the baptism of fire. John the Baptizer declared that Christ would be baptizing people with the Holy Spirit; however, here it is the person of the Holy Spirit who baptizes (1 Cor. 12:13). In one sense, Christ immerses us into the Spirit, enabling us to become empowered believers. In the other, the Holy Spirit baptizes us into Christ's body for the sake of uniting us to him. The baptism into the body precedes the baptism of the Holy Spirit

Baptism into the body happens when we are born again. Without this baptism, there would be no way to receive salvation or any of the spiritual blessings that have been obtained by Christ (Eph. 1:3; 2 Tim. 2:10). As we are united to the Lord, we become beneficiaries of the benefits wrought by his life of obedience to God and death on the cross (Acts 26:18; Rom. 8:17).

In First Corinthians chapter twelve, Paul writes about this baptism. Within his treatment of this subject, he deals with divisions that had arisen within the Church at Corinth due to different gifts. Some felt they were more important while others felt they were insignificant. He writes this amazing passage to show their unity because of this particular baptism (1 Cor. 12:1ff). It is within this passage that we find the only words used by Paul in this way, *"For by one Spirit we were all baptized into one body, whether Jews or Greeks, whether slaves or free, and we were all made to drink of one Spirit"* (1 Cor. 12:13).

The word "baptized" in First Corinthians has a dualistic meaning. The Holy Spirit places us into Christ's body as well as his death because of this baptism. God instantly delivers us from the power of sin through unification with Christ (Rom. 6:3-7). Through baptism into his body, we identify with the complete work that Jesus Christ accomplished on our behalf.

The term "body" is used symbolically to express the practical relationship between Christ and believers (1 Cor. 12:13). This word indicates two things. First, there are multiple parts that must work together in one synchronized movement in order to be productive (1 Cor. 12:12; Eph. 4:16; Col. 2:19) Also, there must be a head – Christ (Eph. 1:22; Col. 1:18). It became the burden of Paul to ensure that these parts maintained unity and submission to the head. Only in this way can the body produce what Christ intended – fruit.

Upon placing your trust in Christ, you identify with four aspects: (A) you are baptized into Christ (Gal. 3:27), (B) you are baptized into his death (Rom. 6:3), (C) you are baptized in his name (Matt. 28:19; Acts 19:5) and (D) you are also baptized into his body (1 Cor. 12:12). Through these four aspects, God unites you to all that Christ is and has accomplished for you.

The Baptism of Suffering

The term baptism of suffering merely indicates is an immersion into an experience of suffering, pain or calamity. This does not mean that your life has to be one of suffering and nothing else. However, it is certain that without this experience, you cannot become a participant in the future kingdom (Acts 14:22).

To form a diamond there must be extreme pressure, temperatures and depth within the Earth. Diamonds develop in temperatures of almost 2000 degrees Fahrenheit and between 90 – 120 miles beneath the Earth's surface. When the diamond has gone through all the changes that are necessary, it becomes one of the most beautiful and the hardest stones in existence.

God wants you to become diamond quality. In order to do this, He has to put you in situations where the temperature rises and the pressure builds. Like the diamond developing in the depth of the Earth, the deeper you go in God, the greater the pressure you will experience. However, these conditions cause you to become hardened and stable. You will be able to bear the weight of anything life has to offer without cracking. If you can handle what God is allowing you to go through, you will become a marvelous specimen for others to behold.

This suffering will only be endured by those who are in the process of maturing (1 Pet. 5:10). Believers who are babes will not endure suffering for an extended period. They need to experience the joy and excitement of the blessed salvation they have received. To thrust spiritual babies into the baptism of suffering to quickly would be detrimental. It would be as the one who receives the Word with joy without it taking root in their lives; consequently, when time of testing comes upon them, they fall away (Matt. 13:5-6, 20- 21).

They do not know how to handle pressure. Instead of trusting God, these babies throw things, curse people out and fight just to name a few. Nonetheless, suffering is a part of the human experience and you must develop the ability to deal with it (Matt. 6:34; 2 Cor. 4:16-18).

When Jesus was on his way to Jerusalem he took his disciples aside to explain to them about the horrible things he was about to suffer which would culminate in his death. As he was sharing this with his disciples, Salome along with her sons, James and John (these two would eventually become reputed leaders in Christianity - Gal. 2:9) took occasion and approached Jesus about positions in his coming kingdom (Mark 10:35). She requested that her sons have the closest positions possible to him – one on the right and one on the left (Mark 10:35-37).

To sit on either the right or the left hand of a ruler showed that the utmost confidence was placed in them (1 Kgs. 2:19; 1 Sam. 20:25; Heb. 1:3). Sitting close to Christ would become a symbol of how great and highly favored her sons would be in the new order.

Although she had a noble request, she was not aware of the requirement to attain to these positions of the highest honor. Jesus responds, *"You do not know what you are asking"* (Mark 10:38). To gain honor in the future kingdom requires that undergo suffering (Acts. 14:22).

The believers who gain privilege in this way have abandoned themselves completely to the cause of Christ. This sacrifice is what Jesus termed as drinking "of the cup". He himself was to endure the most sever baptism which would culminate in him being separated from his Father (Luke 24:46). Therefore, we who would follow him in the future must be willing to undergo our difficulties of suffering.

The word suffering has several references. The first denotes the sensation of pain. It is the internal emotional side of suffering. It is the overwhelming sensation or impression of pain. Some situations that we endure may not affect our body, but send us through the most excruciating mental anguish (Mark 8:31; 1 Pet. 5:10).

Another definition refers to feeling what others feel. It shows the closeness you have with someone else. There are only two places in the Bible where this definition is exemplified. In one passage, it refers to the suffering of Christ's body (1 Cor. 12:26). When one part hurts, we all hurt because we are one body.

The other passage refers to our suffering with Christ. Undergoing some of the same experiences Jesus went through in his humanity guarantees our joint participation with him when he returns to establish his rule (Rom. 8:17). Your relation to Jesus' suffering defines how much glory you will share with him. If you cannot endure the sufferings of Christ Jesus, you will not share in his glory.

Of course, no one looks forward to painful experiences. However, when they come, you should seek to endure them and not just to escape. In order to do this, you must look beyond your days of trouble and understand what you will be gaining – glory (2 Cor. 4:17). Only when you visualize the benefit of suffering can you declare it is easy to handle no matter how difficult it is.

The last meaning pertains to external suffering. It is some type of misfortune or painful experience. This painful experience will come to everyone who follows Christ (2 Cor. 1:5; Heb. 2:10). This is the closest definition to what Christ was referring to when he asked his disciples could they drink of the same cup.

What specifically is this baptism or cup that Jesus was referring to (Matt.20:22)? It was the painful reality of impending physical death. This cup brought him face-to-face with his and his Father's will. Even though he was one with the God, his humanity did not want to experience this aspect of suffering (Matt. 26:38-42).

In fact, he was under such pressure that an angel had to come and strengthen his soul in order for him to continue praying about his future experience on the cross. As he continued to talk to the Father, Jesus underwent such mental anguish and struggles that sweat fell from his face as "great drops of blood" (Luke 22:43, 44). Some theologians believe that this experience was an issue called hematidrosis.

Hematidrosis is the mingling of a person's blood into his perspiration. This is a very dangerous condition usually caused by great strain or stress. Impending physical death definitely fits this category (Matt. 26:38-44; Mark 14:13). Jesus had to come face-to-face with the reality of death and decide that his father's will was more important than his own. This is what Jesus was referring to. You must consider his will more important that your feelings if you will endure the drama coming your way.

Our suffering accomplishes several things:

A. We become obedient to the will of God (Heb. 5:8, 9).

B. We are made into what we should be ethically (1 Pet. 5:10).

C. We gain stability in the faith (1 Pet. 5:9, 10).

D. We gain spiritual knowledge and power (1 Pet. 5:10).

E. We guarantee ourselves to become joint-heirs with Christ (Rom. 8:17).

F. We are able to exhibit the life of Jesus through our everyday living (2 Cor. 4:11).

G. We experience deliverance from a life of sin (1 Pet. 4:1).

H. We can have a joyful expectation of Christ's return (1 Pet. 4:12-13).

I. We are kept humble (2 Cor. 12:9, 10).

J. We are able to be close to Him (Luke 22:28-30).

Ultimately, the baptism of suffering as accomplished through Christ secured all the benefits that came along with having our fellowship restored to God. If we are to experience these benefits subjectively, we must bear our own cross as Jesus bore his (Matt. 16:24f).

The Savior was crucified once for the spiritual freedom and hope of all humanity while we are crucified daily to live in the freedom and hope that he accomplished for us. (Luke 9:23-25). To be associated with Christ in suffering should indeed be considered a privilege because of the fruit it yields (2 Cor. 4:16-17; Philip. 3:10).

The Baptism of the Word

The baptism in the Word is perhaps one of the most obscure aspects of all the baptisms; yet, this is the one that we need to experience daily. Many of God's people have persistent issues with sin and guilt due to an inadequate experience of a daily baptism in the Word. This is the only baptism that deals with the internal aspect of man – his conscience (Heb. 10:22).

The word "washing" is *loutron* in the Greek (Eph. 5:25-27). It speaks of bathing the entire person. Titus 3:5 is the only other place where this word is used. Titus states that salvation comes thru the "washing of regeneration" and the Holy Ghost. This is also called the "laver of regeneration".

The brazen laver foreshadowed the waters of baptism. It was positioned between the altar and the Holy Place and illustrated that people needed cleansing before approaching God. The priests washed before they began their service to Jehovah. In God's New Testament economy, He considers us His priests; therefore, it is with the utmost urgency that we wash ourselves with the Word if we are to handle anything that pertains to God (1 Pet. 2:9; Rev. 1:6).

Washing the hands and feet was symbolic of the priest's actions. Everywhere they went and whatever they did must be pure. Without both bloodshed and cleansing there would be no ministry in the presence of God. To attempt to enter His presence without this process would mean death for every priest (Ex. 30:20). After the application of Christ's blood to our lives, it is imperative that cleansing takes place daily through the Word washing us if we want to serve God in any capacity (John 15:3f).

The baptism of the Word accomplishes a dual purpose. It

serves to "sanctify". This means to purify us from sin. Christ's desire is that we experience deliverance from all that is worldly or sinful. He wants us completely separated from anything that can and will defile.

The second process the Word performs is "cleansing". Along with delivering us from deeds of sin, the Word also delivers us from the guilt of sin. This is the meaning of cleanse. The Word of God cleanses our conscience so that the guilt of sin does not hold us to the past.

Have you ever come out of a situation where you feel like you are forgiven for something that you did in the past but you are held hostage to the past because of the guilt that remains? Jesus wants to deliver you from the sins of your past as well as the guilt associated with them.

Deliverance from sin is one thing. However, if guilt remains, there will continue to be an issue with your conscience. If there is an issue in your conscience, you will have an issue coming before God even though He delivered you from the sin. Guilt will keep you in bondage even though you are no longer living in sin. Jesus has to wash your mind with the Word in order that your past will not hold you captive. Your past ties you to who you were. Jesus is attempting to bring you into who you are supposed to be.

In the Old Covenant, only two things provided cleansing for God's people: the shedding of animal's blood and cleansing with water (Ex. 24:5-8; Lev. 4:1-12; Num. 19:1-18; Ezek. 36:25). These two were types that resembled the cleansing agents of the blood of Christ and the Word of God (Eph. 5:25-27; Heb. 9:14). In the New Testament, only the baptism of the Word and the blood of Jesus provide cleansing.

Many believers neglect this cleansing process because the Word, although it is a cleansing agent, takes them through a process of agitation and irritation. It brings much friction and confrontation to our lives (Jer. 23:29; Heb. 4:12).

If you examine how we wash our physical bodies, clothes, vehicles, etc., you cannot help but notice that there will not be true cleaning without friction. You must apply the cleansing agent with a certain amount of force in order to remove debris, dirt, stains, grease, sweat, dust and tar. The more difficult the stain, the longer the cleaning agent needs to remain on the object.

The most hideous of sins have stained our lives. You and I must meticulously apply the Word of God to our lives on a daily basis if we are going to live in victory. Although this can be an extremely uncomfortable process, the baptism of the Word delivers us from the effects of sin and worldliness.

Through baptism, we undergo several critical experiences, making it possible to minister to and for God. The Spirit baptizes us into Jesus Christ's death for identification. He baptizes us into his body for our union. Finally, we experience daily baptism in the Word for cleansing.

The Baptism for the Dead

The baptism for the dead is a vicarious or proxy baptism. In this substitute baptism, the living person receives baptism on behalf of the dead. Wikipedia states, "Those who practice this rite view baptism as an indispensable requirement to enter the kingdom of God, and thus practiced Baptism for the Dead to give those who have died without ever having had the opportunity to receive baptism the opportunity to receive it by proxy if they wish."[3] In this way, those who are dead have the opportunity to receive baptism, which is indicative of them believing in Jesus Christ, in order that they may enter the kingdom of God. The only reference to this in the Scriptures is in First Corinthians chapter 15 verse 29.

Many theologians agree that this is perhaps one of the most problematic texts to interpret. There are thirty to forty different interpretations of this passage. The passage reads, *"What will those do who are baptized for the dead? If the dead are not raised at all, why then are they baptized for them?"*

It is difficult to interpret this passage as referring to believers baptized on the behalf of those who are already dead in order that Christ will bring these deceased ones into fellowship with him. Although some other religions believe in proxy baptisms, two things make this scenario highly unlikely.

First, Jesus was the only one enabled to stand on behalf of others to accomplish something that has eternal significance. He died on the cross for every man; now, each individual must decide for themselves to accept what Jesus accomplished **before** they die.

Second, when a person dies, God categorizes them as believer or unbeliever. We cannot change our destiny after death has occurred. The Scripture clearly states, *"It is appointed for men to die once and after this comes judgement..."* (Heb. 9:27). One who understands the future judgements can speedily agree with my position. Brother Toney Warren declares two other reasons why this interpretation is difficult to process:

1. "We not only have a doctrine which is nowhere else

spoken of in all of Scripture, but we force God to introduce an entirely new subject into this context 'with only this one sentence,' and then never speaks of it again anywhere."

2. "We have a doctrine which is contradictory to the rest of the Bible. The Holy Bible declares very unambiguously that it is impossible for one to be saved without faith in Jesus Christ as Savior. No one after death can be saved by the action of someone who is alive."

He further writes, "The teaching that men can be saved merely by an act of another man participating in water baptism, is not only unbiblical (John 14:6), it is anti-biblical."[4] It is **impossible** for anyone to come into fellowship with the Father apart from personally placing their faith in Jesus Christ before they die.

Other viewpoints of this verse include:

A. The church father Epiphanius believed that this refers to teaching people about the future resurrection while they lay upon their deathbed.

B. Others believe that this refers to baptism for other believers who were outside the church.

C. The last option is that this text refers to those who are willing to be associated with Christ and are willing to suffer the similar trials of those who have lived before them. They are persuaded of the resurrection and are thereby baptized.[5]

Not far from Corinth was a city called Eleusis. There were pagan religions that practiced proxy baptisms. They believed this would have an effect on a person's destiny in the after-life. It is quite probable that the Christian Corinthian citizen saw the practices of their neighbors and decided to do the same. Paul had to correct such errors.

There are other evidences that people practiced this method during the early centuries of the Church. In 393a.d. there was a synod hosted in Hippo Regius located in northern Africa. It declares that, "The Eucharist shall not be given to dead bodies, nor baptism conferred upon them. The ruling was confirmed four years later in the sixth canon of the Third Council of Carthage."[6] Since the spiritual leaders mentioned this in their councils, there must have been significant participation in this practice.

Most of the Church rejected the baptism of the dead. It is very apparent that this practice opposes the Bible. By studying this baptism, we can be sure that people believed in the resurrection and life after death. It should become our burden to preach Christ to people before they die to ensure they have the proper chance to place their faith in Christ, and subsequently baptized.

Other Washings

As we have studied various baptisms, we must keep in perspective that the author to the Hebrews was a Hebrew writing from a Hebraic perspective. In order to get a holistic point of view concerning baptism, we must understand the significance of washings under the Mosaic order (Heb. 9:8-10).

There are two important things to note about this term "various washings". First, it is a term which refers to the washings prescribed under the Mosaic Law. Such practices had become obsolete for those who experience baptizism into the body of Christ.

Second, the Greek word for washings (baptismos) is also

the same word for baptism. The washings of the Old Testament were actuality baptisms. The author wanted to make a contrast between the "various washings" under the old covenant and the "baptisms" of the new. This is why the writer of Hebrews mentions "various washings" in Hebrews chapter 9 and 10.

According to Hebrews 9:10, there was a limited time for the Jews to practice this system of washings under the Old Covenant which was until God made improvements after the death of His son. The old system of washings was incomplete (Lev. 14:8, 17:15). Although it was able to make the external clean, it was useless in dealing with man's conscience (Num. 8:6, 7; Matt. 23:25-28). Only after the death of the Messiah could this system be rectified through the sprinkling of his blood upon the conscience of man (Heb. 10:22). This would become the perfect order of things.

Under the Law, the other way of cleansing was also with the use of the blood of animals. It was sprinkled around the altar, upon the priests, their garments, before the veil of the sanctuary and upon lepers (Ex. 29:16-21; Lev. 4:6, 14:6, 7).

The sprinkling in the Old Testament foreshadowed the fact that Christ, after his death, would take the role of high priest on our behalf and sprinkle his blood upon the mercy seat to obtain God's pardon. This sprinkling of the blood would be applied to our conscience in order that we may have confidence before God living a productive life for him (Heb. 9:11-14, 10:19-25).

The comparison here is that the sprinkling of the Old Testament cleansed the outside of things whereas the blood of Jesus cleanses our conscience from the guilt of sin, in order that we may serve him.

The doctrine of baptisms encompasses key events that will happen in everyone's life. While most of these pertain to what God desires to do in believers, the baptism of fire remains the worst experience everyone will have who refuses to surrender their lives to God.

LAYING ON OF HANDS

The hands are used for many things such as feeling, receiving, holding objects and communicating, but we need to understand the purpose of "laying on the hands" concerning the principle here. The laying on of hands was a very significant aspect in the daily affairs of the Israelites, the ministry of Jesus and is in the operation of the Church today.

The imposition of hands is so important to the New Testament economy that it is included as a part of the basic doctrine concerning Christ (Heb. 6:2). This is why the writer to the Hebrews considered this principle to be part of the ABC's concerning Christ. With all of the examples in the Bible of people laying their hand on someone, we can see that it had mainly three functions: consecration, impartation of a divine gift, and identification with a sacrifice. These elements are important because they make the giver or offender one with whom they are dealing.

When I say giver or offender, I mean that the person whom is imparting something spiritual into another is a giver, whereas, those who committed sins, laying their hand on the head of the offering as a means of identifying with it are offenders.

IMPLEMENTATION IN THE OLD TESTAMENT

Laying the Hand on the Thigh

For the most part, the people laid their hand on someone's

head, but there are a couple of incidents where someone placed their hand upon another individual's thigh.Placing the hand upon the thigh symbolized strength and covenant (Gen. 24:9). Coupled with this, the person usually invoked the name of God. Such was the case with Abraham when he was sending his servant to find a wife for Isaac.

The narrative in Genesis tells us that when Abraham was old, he desired to find a wife for his son. He sent Eliezer, his oldest servant out but made him make an oath before he left (Gen. 24:1-9). Eliezer based his oath upon the self-existence of God who ruled the heavens and Earth and violation of it would have severe consequences. The only other instance where this type of oath is used is when Jacob asked Joseph to swear about taking his body out of Egypt when Israel left (Gen. 47:29).

Blessing Others

Genesis chapter 48 is the first time we see hands laid upon an individual in an act of blessing. Someone brings Joseph news that his father Jacob was sick, and apparently at the point of death, because he rushed to his father immediately bringing with him his two sons, Manasseh and Ephraim (Gen. 48:14ff).

Joseph was aware that when a child's father was about to pass away, they would pronounce a blessing upon them which was both spiritual and physical (Gen. 27:1-4). What the father spoke usually manifested in the years that followed. This is what happened when Jacob laid his hands upon his grandchildren.

I would approach this very cautiously. I remember when one of my former pastors was talking to the congregation. He said that when he laid his hands on someone, whatever he said would (he placed great emphasis on the word "would") come to pass as if he could not make any error in what he said concerning someone's life. People can say all kinds of things for many reasons including just simply being in the flesh. Therefore, not everything spoken over you will come to pass.

Offerings

This is highly significant because here is where people laid their hands for the purpose of identification. People laid their hands upon the head of the sacrifice in two offerings. These were the peace and sin offering. Some theologians believe that during the sin offering, the one who gave the animal as a sacrifice placed their hand upon the sacrifice in order to transfer their guilt of sin. Others disagree with this perspective. They believe that only the scapegoat was symbolic of the releasing of the sins (Lev. 16:21, 22).

Aaron was to lay both his hands upon the scapegoat confessing the sins of Israel. Once he laid his hands upon the goat, the sins transferred to it. This goat would be released into the wilderness bearing "upon him all their iniquities" (Lev. 16:8-10). Once Aaron placed his hands upon the scapegoat, he would make a declaration of atonement for him and the nation. With this act, he was not only acknowledging his sins and those of the nation, but by putting his hands on the animal, Aaron identified with it, as it became their vicarious appeasement to God. This scapegoat represented none other than Jesus Christ, who knew no sin, but became sin for us (1 Cor. 5:21). God released us from our sins by judging Christ on the cross.

The burnt offering was similar to the sin offering (Lev. 1:4). The priest accomplished the burnt offering with either a bull or ram. The people of the congregation put their hands on this bull, which represented that the people sinned continuously; consequently, there must be a continuous offering to appease the judgement of God (Num. 28:3).

Aaron and the priest also laid their hands upon the ram of the burnt offering (Ex. 29:19-28; Lev. 3:2). Ancient customs lead us to believe that the breast of the ram, used as a wave offering, was waved from side to side; while the thigh, used as a heave offering, was present in an up and down motion thus making a symbol of the cross. Upon this cross, Christ became our peace offering. The laying on of hands upon this ram indicated that humanity understood their need for a peace offering to appease the wrath of God.

Ordination

There was a special service held for the Levites to consecrate them for service. God told Moses to have them purified by sprinkling the water of the sin offering upon them. They were also to remove all hair from their flesh. Next, they were to wash their clothes. After this, they were to have both a meat and sin offering. The next step was the laying on of hands, by the entire congregation of Israel (Num. 8:6-10).

When the Bible speaks of "the entire congregation", this must have been a select few. It would have been physically impossible for the entire congregation to touch them seeing their numbers added to over one million. Some believe these people were the first-born of Israel since the Levites would replace the requirement of the firstborn to be dedicated to God (Num. 8:16-18).

Others believe these were the princes who gave their

blessing to them. The important thing to note here is that this was a group of individuals who laid their hands upon the Levites, not a single person. I believe this needed to be a corporate effort because the Levites would represent all Israel in performing service in the tent of meeting and later the temple (1 Chr. 23:1-6).

Installing a National Leader

When Moses' time for leading the children of Israel was concluding, he asked God to select someone who could continue to lead the Israelites. God's appointed man was Joshua. God instructed Moses to lay his hands upon him in the presence of the congregation (Num. 27:15-23).

Moses touched Joshua, imparting some of his honor when he commissioned him (Deut. 31:23). The book of Deuteronomy records that Joshua was *"...filled with the spirit of wisdom, for Moses had laid his hands on him..."* (Deut. 34:9).This is the first instance where we can see the laying on of hands used to impart something spiritual unto another person.

Passing Judgement

There is one instance in the Bible where people put their hands upon a person who was being judged because of his transgression (Lev. 24:10-14). There was a person of mixed descent who lived among the Israelites. His mother was an Israelite while his father was an Egyptian. This young man ended up in strife with another person who was a pure Israelite. The sources of this rift are not declared. What we do know is that the person whose father was an Egyptian cursed the Israelite's God. His sin was so grievous that those who heard the argument brought him directly to

Moses for judgement.

After seeking God about what should be done, those who heard his blasphemy were instructed to bring him outside of the camp, lay their hands upon him and inflict punishment through stoning. This made the penalty of the person legal while at the same time indicating that this half-blooded Israelite was responsible for his own sin (Lev. 24:15).

IMPLEMENTATION IN THE NEW TESTAMENT

The act of laying hands has been implemented in the New Testament. The same basic concept is kept except the sacrificial system has been abolished. According to The International Standard Bible Encyclopedia, the only thing that changes in the New Testament is when the presbytery laid their hand on someone there was the accompaniment of spiritual gifts.

The laying on of hands by Jesus was a very common way that Jesus used to bless and pray for people. While Jesus touched some people, others touched him (Mark 10:16; Luke 6:19). Whether people touched Jesus or vice versa, the power of the point of contact is undeniable. Contact inspires faith.

This is why many times when preachers pray for people after the preached, they lay their hands on them. Often times, at this point of contact, people will begin to cry and surrender their heart to God. The contact helps people release their faith.

Healing

Jesus gave the disciples the ability to lay their hands on sick people in order that they might experience healing (Mark 16:17, 18). Jesus gave this special capability to them in order that those who saw these deeds would believe that God sent these men. Others laid their hands on people for the expressed purposed of invoking the healing power of God (Acts 28:8; James 5:14).

There was a man in the book of Acts, disabled from the time of his birth, who sat daily at the entrance of the temple gate called Beautiful begging for money (Acts 3:1ff). One particular day, Peter and John saw him sitting there as they went to the temple to pray. Peter did not have any money to give this man; however, he had faith to believe God for healing. He prayed for him, took hold of the impotent man, imparting healing in his body; thus, enabling him to walk.

We do not have power within our hands. However, we become the vessel that God uses to release His power. Like copper wire being a conduit for electricity, believers who have an intimate relationship with God become a channel for which God can release His power through.

Ordaining Elders and Deacons

During the early stages of the Church, it is recorded that the number of the disciples began to increase exponentially (Acts 2:41-47). As the amount of converts grew, there began to be a disagreement between the Grecian and Hebrew disciples. The Grecian believers felt Jewish widows received better service than theirs (Acts 6:1-6).

The twelve apostles did not want to leave their devotion to the ministry of the Word to feed widows. Instead, they purposed that the disciples find seven individuals for this service who were of "good reputation" and "full of the Spirit and of wisdom".

The disciples presented these believers to the apostles

who, after laying their hands, installed them as the main servants to the widows. The laying of the hands also showed that the apostles identified and agreed with the choice of the other disciples.

Further along in the book of Acts, we see the commissioning of Paul and Barnabas for missionary work (Acts 13:3). After diligently fasting and praying, the Spirit of God spoke to the prophets and teachers, instructing them to separate Paul and Barnabas to ordain them for service. After further fasting and praying, carefully considering the will of God, these leaders laid their hands on these two men, sending them out as workers in the ministry.

Timothy was admonished to remember everything that was placed in him for the administration of the office of an evangelist (1 Tim. 4:14; 2 Tim. 1:6). There was an installation meeting in which Paul, along with other elders, imparted to Timothy a certain gift by the laying on of hands. Outside of laying hands to pray for healing, using this process to ordain leaders and elders is the next most commonly practiced action.

Helping Others Receive the Holy Spirit

There was a great revival that occurred in Samaria because of the preaching of the evangelist Philip (Acts 8). The news concerning this recovery reached the ears of the apostles in Jerusalem. The leadership sent Peter and John, who laid their hands upon the new converts, helping them receive the Holy Spirit (Acts 8:17).

Performing Signs and Wonders

Signs and Wonders are different from works of healing. Signs are events that take place, which goes against the common course of nature such as when Jesus turned water into wine. These are usually done for the purpose of authenticating that certain people are the servants of God or that there message is really God sent (Matt. 12:38; 1 Cor. 1:22). A wonder is more of a miracle in general. Both of these are significantly exhibited in the Church (1 Cor. 12:10, 28).

When Paul and Barnabas were in Iconium evangelizing, many listening believed their preaching. However, some of the Jews were able to convince a portion of the Gentiles to think corruptly about the godly words of these two men (Acts 14:1, 2). Therefore, they needed to remain in Iconium for a long time, working to convince as many of the Gentiles as possible about salvation. To help authenticate their message, God allowed them to work signs and wonders through the imposition of their hands (Mark 16:20; Acts 19:11).

THE ADMONITION

There is one verse in the Bible warning about the laying on of hands. It states, *"Do not lay hands upon anyone too hastily..."* (1 Tim. 5:22). This verse has to do specifically with the imposition of hands for ordination of a person. There is to be an extreme examination of the person introduced into the ministry (1 Tim. 3:1-16).

If a leader lays their hands on anyone with a life defiled by sin, they in effect become partakers of this person's sin. In laying hands on them, you actually give approval to their life. This must not be so. Instead, we are admonished to rebuke those who have sin in their lives (1 Tim. 5:20).

The imposition of hands for the installation of a person in service is a solemn event and must remain pure. Let this be a strong warning against any leader who would install any person in service knowing that their lives indicate they should hold no position in ministry. It is your responsibility to make sure they qualify to have hands laid on them. By doing this, we will ensure the integrity of this process.

THE RESURRECTION OF THE DEAD

First Corinthians chapter 15 is Paul's Magna Carta on the resurrection. Of the six principles we are discussing, the resurrection of the dead takes pre-eminence above them all. Without a resurrection, there is no need to discuss any of these principles. In fact, it is the resurrection that completes the gospel (1 Cor. 15:1-4).

The doctrine of the resurrection is so indispensable to the Christian faith that it is clearly written about, or at least alluded to in almost every New Testament book. Even scriptures that refer to Christ's return or second coming preclude his resurrection. Most importantly, Jesus declared that he was the author of resurrection (John 11:25). This is the good news of the gospel.

In this chapter Paul is also referring to the orders of the resurrection and the type of bodies we will have after the resurrection. This is a full complex chapter and may take some time to comprehend. It is necessary to understand the resurrection because what you believe about tomorrow affects how you live today.

THE RESURRECTION COMPLETES THE GOSPEL

As you study the word "gospel" you will find that it means "good news" or "glad tidings" (1 Cor. 15:1). I ask how a preacher can declare glad tidings or good news concerning Christ merely coming and dying. This would not be grounds for rejoicing. If Jesus had only died, he would not have accomplished the complete will of God to affect our eternal destiny. The fact that he was raised from the dead and ascended into heaven to complete the work of redemption is what gives every Christian grounds to declare that the message of Jesus Christ is indeed good news.

According to First Corinthians, the gospel that Paul presented contained three elements: (1) Christ died for our sins, (2) He was buried and (3) He experienced resurrection (1 Cor. 15:3, 4). Even our Lord himself, when he spoke of his work of redemption always concluded it with the reality that he would be resurrected (Matt. 20:17-20). If you do not believe in Jesus Christ's death, burial and resurrection, you do not believe in the full gospel.

If the saints at Corinth did not believe in the resurrection, Paul stated they would depart from the truth (1 Cor. 15:1). We live in a day and time that many teach truths contradicting the complete gospel of Jesus Christ. It requires proper fellowship with the Lord and others to enable you to hold fast the teachings you have received concerning Christianity.

Verse two in chapter fifteen contains two key phrases: "you are saved" and "hold fast". The phrase "you are saved" literally means "you are being saved". As you continue to believe in the entire gospel, you position yourself to continue in the process of salvation from error, corrupt notions and moral impurity (1 Tim. 4:1, 2). The resurrection validates everything Jesus accomplished in his humanity.

Progressive salvation pertains to what God is doing in your soul. The resurrection is a harness for the way you think and what you do. The validity of the resurrection of our Savior is the reason why you can persevere in your salvation.

Paul said that they needed to "hold fast" the gospel that he communicated to them. If we think of grasping something, we think of a clinched or closed fist. The tighter the grasp on something, the more secure it becomes. The Corinthians as do you and I needed to keep the complete gospel secured with their minds in order that it may not be removed from them by any would be thieves (1 Tim. 6:20, 21).

The resurrection and ascension are the concluding acts to Jesus' redemptive work in his humanity, which affects everything about our present and future. Therefore, Paul continues writing to the Corinthians in chapter fifteen dealing with the resurrection event.

Some will declare that, "There is no need to know about the elements of the resurrection of the dead. We will find out about our bodies and the order of the resurrection when the time comes." I would reply that if the author of the epistle to the Hebrews believed that this principle was important enough to include it in the ABC's of the doctrine of Christ, then the reality of the resurrection must have some significant impact on your life right now.

THE REALITY OF HIS RESURRECTION

The resurrection of Jesus Christ is a fact. According to the Scripture and other sources, he made as many as twelve post resurrection appearances:

1. He appeared first to Mary Magdalene (Mark 16:9)

2. He appeared to the women returning from the tomb (Matt. 28:9-10)

3. He appeared to two disciples on the road to Emmaus (Luke 24:13)

4. He appeared to Peter in Jerusalem (Luke 24:34; 1 Cor. 15:5)

5. He appeared to the disciples and others. Thomas was not present. (Luke 24:36-43; John 20:19-23)

6. He appeared a week later to his disciples behind locked doors. This time Thomas was present (John 20:24-29).

* This is when Jesus gave them the indwelling Spirit for eternal life (vs. 22).

7. He appeared to seven of his disciples on the shore of the Sea of Galilee (John 21:1-24).

8. He appeared to five hundred believers at one time (1 Cor. 15:6).

9. He appeared to James (1 Cor. 15:7).

10. He appeared to eleven disciples on a mountain in Galilee (Matt. 28:18-20).

11. He walked with his disciples along the road to Bethany, and then ascended into Heaven (Luke 24:50-53).

* I believe this process of Jesus showing himself took approximately 40 days (Acts 1:1-3).

12. He appeared to Paul on the road to Damascus (Acts 9:3-6; 1 Cor. 15:8).[1]

If Jesus felt the need to show himself this many times, then his resurrection must have been very significant.

WHAT IF THERE WAS NO RESURRECTION

If there is no resurrection, we have a significant problem. In his great treaties on the resurrection, Paul gives a few reasons as to what the scenario would be if God does not raise the dead.

1. If there is no resurrection, Christ has not been raised (1 Cor. 15:13). This would be disastrous for every believer. If God did not raise Christ, then the complete work of salvation was not accomplished.

2. The proclamation of all who are heralds of the gospel is useless (1 Cor. 15:14). "Preaching" is not the general communication of truth. This declaration pertains to the efforts of evangelism. It is the proclaiming that Christ has accomplished salvation. However, this would be a lie if there is no resurrection of the dead.

3. We have placed our faith in the wrong individual (1 Cor. 15:14). Believing that Jesus Christ is the Messiah who has enabled us to participate in God's eternal kingdom would be the greatest lie.

4. We are lying about our experiences concerning God (1 Cor. 15:15). The word "testified" means to speak about something based upon your experience. If there is no resurrection, then Paul was lying about everything he heard, saw and experienced due to God's divine presence and revelation

5. We are still in our sins (1 Cor. 15:17). There would be no peace in a believer's life. All humankind should expect to experience the wrath of God due to their sinful condition.

6. Those who died as Christians are actually gone into eternal perdition (1 Cor. 15:18). The only judgement to be experienced is God sending everyone to the lake of fire.

If God did not raise Jesus Christ, we have a major problem. The great news is that he has risen from the dead. The resurrection of Jesus did happen.

BECAUSE THERE IS A RESURRECTION

The resurrection did however take place. Because God raised Christ, there were benefits given to believers that I am quite positive we cannot fully comprehend in this present life. These include:

1. The imparting of the Holy Spirit (John 16:4f, 20:19-23). In chapter 16 of the gospel of John, Jesus is speaking to his disciples concerning the coming of the Holy Spirit. This is the great teacher's last topic he discussed with the disciples before his arrest.

Jesus told his followers that he purposefully left these words for last, *"These things I did not say to you at the beginning, because I was with you"* (John16:4b). The Lord speaks now of the Holy Spirit because it is time for his departure back to the Father.

As great a sage as Jesus was he could not reside inside believers nor was he omniscient due to the physical limitations of his human body. However, as the Spirit, he could be with everyone who relies upon his help, comfort and guidance.

The Holy Spirit enables you to come into a deeper knowledge of the truth concerning Christ, as well as help you deal with your life's issues successfully. The Holy Spirit accomplishes the work of Christ in the lives of believers on a broader perspective.

2. The resurrection proved Jesus' identity (Rom. 1:4). By this, I do not mean the Jesus Christ was not already God's

divine son. Scripture is clear that he was (John 1:18). Yet, Jesus had to go through resurrection because he was clothed with a human nature (John 1:14).

Even though Christ was divine in his nature, God had to deal with his humanity. Through the resurrection process, God openly declared him, in his humanity, as the divine Son. The resurrection is what separates Jesus from every other great teacher or prophet in history.

3. The resurrection of Jesus was proof that the Holy Spirit has power to give us a resurrection body (Rom. 8:11). All believers are given the Spirit as a pledge that God will raise the body (Eph. 1:13, 14). Yes, there will be a resurrection for everyone who dies; however, the indication in the book of Romans is that our resurrection will occur because God raised Jesus Christ.

4. Through the resurrection, God assures everyone of a future judgement (Acts 17:31). The prior verse in Acts tells us that God has commanded us to repent, whereas verse thirty-one tells us why (Acts 17:30). God has determined a day when Christ will judge the Earth. Paul shows in Acts chapter seventeen that although Christ was delivered to death, God raised him up proving that Jesus Christ will become the judge of the entire Earth (1 Sam. 2:10).

5. The resurrection shows Christ's power over death and the grave (Acts 2:23, 24; 1Cor. 15:55-57). The death, burial and resurrection of Christ Jesus were not accidental. God prearranged and appointed Christ's body, the timing of his birth and his enemies that would turn him over to a vicious, brutal and bloody death (1 Cor. 2:8). Although God determined that Jesus would have to die as our unblemished sacrifice, his body would not decay in the tomb (Ps. 16:8-11; Acts 2:26-28).

Death, as our enemy, held people in bondage. Jesus Christ, through his resurrection, reigned over death. He could not be held by it because he had life within himself and never experienced sin (John 6:35, 2 Cor. 5:21). Jesus knew he was going to rise from the dead. He concluded that, *"You have made known to me the ways of life; you will make me full of gladness with your presence"* (Acts 2:28).

The "ways of life" refers to Jesus' post-resurrection life. He knew that God would resurrect him from the dead, bringing him back to the place of his origin. As a consequence, he would experience the greatest joy. Christ conquered death and the grave. He will never experience death again. It is fitting that the concluding words of First Corinthians chapter fifteen are *"...Death is swallowed up in victory. O death, where is your victory? O death, where is your sting?"* (1 Cor. 15:54b, 55). Now we have confidence that we will be raised from our sleep (1 Thes. 4:14).

6. Through his resurrection, Christ delivered those who were captives in Hades. It was the holding place of the righteous as well as the wicked who died prior to the crucifixion (Luke 16:19-31; Eph. 4:8).

Christ took into custody believers who were prisoners of death, leading them in a processional to heaven (Eph. 4:8, 9). Before he ascended, we are told that he descended into the "lower parts of the Earth", known as Hell or Hades.Paul understood this transferring of souls. He knew that now to be "absent from the body" is to "be at home with the Lord" (2 Cor. 5:8).

7. After his resurrection and ascension, our Lord gave gifts to his body (Eph. 4:8). These gifts are not those invested in the life of an individual for the use of ministering to people. Those are called "spiritual gifts" (1

Cor. 12:4-7).

These gifts in Ephesians are actually people. Christ desired so much that we become spiritually mature, that he invested special people into his body. Paul specifically identified these individuals in Ephesians chapter four verse eleven. They are called apostles, prophets, evangelists, pastors and teachers.

Not everyone can fill these offices. As the Scripture states, he gave **some** individuals to the body to fill these offices. There will be no spiritual growth without these "gifts".

8. Jesus' resurrection became our grounds to receive forgiveness of sins (Eph. 2:5, 6). The work which God accomplished through the resurrection of Christ allowed us to be freed from sin and its penalty which was death; consequently, the lake of fire (Rev. 20:14, 15).

9. Jesus' resurrection became our guarantee that we would be justified (Rom. 4:25). According to the Scriptures, as we believed into Christ, God declared that we were free from the guilt and penalty of sin. Christ's resurrection made provision for God to declare you righteous when you placed your faith in his Son.

10. Christ's resurrection also enables all believers to be delivered from the impending wrath of God (1 Thes. 1:10). This begins with God's punishment on the rebellious and sinful persons during the "day of wrath" and concludes with his judgement of the unjust at the great white throne (Rom. 2:5-8; Rev. 20:11-15). This is different from the tribulation period, which unleashes of the "wrath of the devil" (Rev. 11:2, 12:12).

THE RAPTURE

The rapture is not the same as the resurrection although the resurrection will be included the process. This word rapture is not in the Bible but is a literal event that Christians believe will take place in the future.

Rapture simply indicates a mode of transporting. During the first phase of Christ's second coming, he will descend from heaven with the spirits of the saints who have already past uniting them with their body while simultaneously removing the living righteous from the Earth to meet him in the air (1 Thes. 4:16, 17). This is the first aspect of his second coming.

People throughout generations have discussed the timing of this event in relation to the tribulation. Although there are differences of opinions as to when this event will occur, nearly everyone believes that it will happen at some point in time. There are three primary views. The first is known as the pre-tribulation viewpoint. Proponents of this perspective believe that the rapture will take place **before** the tribulation. They believe that the Church will not experience the wrath of God and therefore will not experience any part of the tribulation (1 Thes. 5:9).

The second group believes that the rapture will occur approximately **mid-way** through the tribulation. The reason why the supporters of this perspective think the saints will be raptured midway into the tribulation is because they don't believe the church is going to experience any part of the tribulation.

There is a seven year peace pact that the Antichrist makes but breaks it midway. This would be 3 ½ years. Since the tribulation only lasts 3 ½ years, the church must be removed before this time of trouble begins.

They base their view upon the book of Daniel. In 7:21, 22, he writes about the Antichrist prevailing against and wearing out the saints until Christ physically returned to deliver them. The duration of his victory would last *"a time and times and half a time"*. This is equivalent to three and one half years, 1260 days or 42 months. Since many believe that the tribulation will last seven years, this would be the mid-way point (Dan. 7:25; Rev. 12:6, 4).

The last group of people are post-tribulation proponents. They believe that the rapture of the saints occurs **after** the tribulation. Although they are few in number, some people do believe the church will experience the tribulation in its totality. However, this is the least accepted viewpoint, and it finds little support in the Scriptures other than Matthew 24:29-31.

THE RESURRECTION EVENT

The resurrection is defined as "a rising from death" or "a standing up again". Resurrection is different from the rapture. It speaks primarily to bringing one back to life while the rapture deals the removal of those who are alive as well as dead (1 Thes. 4:16, 17). The resurrection includes everyone while the rapture pertains only to believers. There are multiple significant resurrections and the Bible. We will discuss these later.

THE BIBLICAL HARVESTING MODEL

When the farmers plant seed, there are three aspects of the removal of the crop. Some of the harvest ripens early. These are the first fruits. The first fruits are the guarantee that there will be a future harvest. After the harvest of the first fruits, what remains to come is the general harvest. Finally, there is the gleaning (Lev. 19:9; 23:10, 22). The gleanings are what remain after the general harvest has occurred. The resurrection will take place just like the harvest event.

In his writing, Paul uses the metaphor of a harvest to show how the resurrection will occur. The first fruits (Christ, the Old Testament saint, the Church) will be the first group of individuals to experience the resurrection. Next will be the general harvest (the remaining portion of the Church). Finally, the gleaning (the tribulation saints). These elements are of extreme importance because of the order in which God has ordained the process of the resurrection to occur.

THE ORDER OF THE RESURRECTION

As you read First Corinthians chapter fifteen, you will find that the resurrection has a process to it. The passage reads *"But each in his own order: Christ the first fruits, after that those who are Christ's at His coming, then comes the end…"* (1 Cor. 15:23, 24a). The resurrection is not some random act of God. It is a very methodical procedure. God will systematically raise every person in a particular order.

Notice the words "own order". These are two extremely important words. The word "own" means "harmonizing with, suitable; assigned to one's nature, character, aims, acts or that which is appropriate". The word "order" means "that which has been arranged, thing placed in order, a body of soldiers, a band, troop or class, **a series or succession.**"[2]

From these two words, we see that God has first

designed the resurrection to occur in a series or classification. Second, this categorization centers upon a person's nature, character and their actions while they lived upon this Earth. God does not haphazardly raise everyone simultaneously. He does it in a series of succession. God evaluates your nature, character and the way you lived your life.

Based upon His knowledge about your life, He raises you in a particular series. The more your character has been conformed to that of Christ's, the earlier you will be resurrected. The people who are least conformed will stay in the ground the longest. This is why it behooves you to live a life pleasing to God. This will ensure your participation in the early series of the resurrection.

You can have two saints at the same service shouting over the same message. However, when the resurrection occurs God raises one saint before the other. How could this be? God knows what each person's nature and character is like. The external may appear the same but the internal has a great deal of difference. God took note of how each one was living outside of church service. This makes all the difference in the world.

Everyone who died will participate in the resurrection. Yet, God raises some sooner while others He raises others later. The sooner you are raised, the more benefits God gives you in the after-life.

There will be three different groups who will partake in this process. These include Christ, Believers and Unbelievers. The resurrection and rapture of believers will consist of: (A) the rapture of the Church, (B) the resurrection of righteous Israel (C) the resurrection of the tribulation saints and (D) the resurrection of the millennial saints.

Christ

In the scope of this end-time harvesting, Christ is the first fruits (Lev. 23:10; 1 Cor. 15:20, 23). In Leviticus, there was a sheaf of the first fruits presented to the priest. This sheaf was a portion of the first fruits. This represented Jesus Christ. The Lord must become the first partaker of this process because he is to have pre-eminence in all things (Col. 1:18).

As stated before, the resurrection will happen in a series. Those who participate in a particular sequence will do so because of their nature, character, and deeds. Christ clearly is incomparable in all three areas; consequently, he was the first to be recalled to life.

Overcoming Believers

We now turn to ponder the first-fruit catching away of overcomers from both the O.T. saints and the Church. Jesus Christ is **the** first fruits of all the harvest. However, when the time of the harvesting begins for believers, there are other first fruits (Ex. 23:19; Lev. 23:10-11, 15-17).

The word "first fruits" only pertains to three things outside of Christ. These are: (A) produce (Ex. 23:16; Lev. 23:10ff; Deut. 18:4), (B) money and other substance (Prov. 3:9), (C) Israel (Jer. 2:3; Rom. 8:23), (D) the first individuals added to the Church in a particular location (Rom. 16:5; James 1:18) and **(E) the overcomers – special ones of Israel and the Church removed from the Earth and presented to God.** The Bible clearly differentiates these individuals from the rest of the harvest (Rev. 14:4).

The first fruits recorded in Leviticus 23 represent those of Israel and the Church who matured beyond all others.

These individuals lived their lives in a way that excelled the status quo, growing in their spiritual life and acquiring knowledge enabling them to understand mysteries discerned by only a few. In short, their fellowship with God was tremendous.

After the sheaf of first fruits was presented to the priest, there was the remainder of the first fruits (Lev. 23:10-11). Who are these first fruits? Some theologians believe these represent the overcoming Saints of the Old Testament. They believe these are the individuals who were resurrected in Mathew chapter 27 verses 51 through 53. Out of all the believers who died under the old covenant, only a few graves were opened. These graves were symbolic of those considered first fruits of the Old Testament.

Further along in Leviticus, there is another mention of first fruits (Lev. 23:15-17) these are not the same as those mentioned in verses 10 and 11. The first fruits of the harvest verses 10 and 11 were presented to the priest whereas the first fruits of verses 15 through 17 were presented to the Lord. A careful examination of the Scripture will reveal that the first fruits in verses 15 to 17 were harvested at Pentecost representing the church age. There are overcomers in every generation.

God never leaves Himself without witness. There will always be people in every place who declare their faithfulness to God. The first fruits represent the best portion of believers. The book of Revelation chapter 14 records the characteristics of these special ones:

1. They stood upon Mount. Zion. This speaks of heaven, which is the antitype of Jerusalem.

2. They number 144,000. This is not the same group of

144,000 found in chapter 7. There, an angel seals 12,000 individuals from among each tribe of Israel, preserving them during the time of the great tribulation. They are not "redeemed" they are "preserved". In addition, the 144,000 in chapter 14 is symbolic not literal.

3. The angels seal them in their foreheads, indicating that they belonged to God, as opposed to those having the mark of the beast (Rev. 14:9).

4. They were singing praises before the throne.

5. They were not *"defiled with women, for they have kept themselves chaste."* (Rev. 14:4). The first fruits keep themselves pure from sin and idolatry (2 Cor. 11:2).

6. They *"follow the Lamb wherever He goes"* meaning they are his most loyal and truest disciples (Rev. 14:4).

7. They stand faultless before the throne of God (Col. 1:22; Jude 1:24).

8. These individuals have become so dear to God that He removes them from the Earth to keep them from experiencing any miseries that will be forthcoming in the tribulation.

The listed characteristics show why these were superior to all other believers. God did not have respect of persons. These people **proved to God** that they were special, as such; God removed them from the Earth as a special offering to himself (Rev. 12:5).

If you believe that God will not remove some people from the Earth while leaving others behind, I implore you to think again. There is plenty of evidence in the Bible that suggests God intends to remove some people from the Earth while leaving others. Do you remember Enoch? He was so dear to God that the Bible says, *"And Enoch walked with God; and he was not, for God took him"* (Gen. 5:24). God was so pleased with Enoch's life that He would not let his servant physically die, so he removed him from the Earth (Heb. 11:5). God did not translate the rest of his family though.

Elijah also experienced a special rapture. As he walked with his protégé Elisha, conversing with him, a chariot of fire came, separating them from each other, rapturing Elijah while Elisha remained (2Kgs. 2:11). I am not saying that Elisha was not in right standing with God. I am merely showing you that some people are so dear to God that He will take them while leaving others behind.

Concerning the Church, God removes the overcomers from the Earth before the tribulation begins, while rapturing the rest of the Church sometime later. This is known as a "split rapture". Another passage in the Bible speaks about this special removal.

In Matthew chapter 24, Jesus discusses the issue of the time of the great tribulation (Matt.24:29). The Lord speaks about two men and women working in the field. He then makes a statement indicating that one of them is removed from the Earth, while the other is left behind (Matt. 24:40, 41). From this passage, it appears this first fruits rapture happens prior to the "great tribulation".

Jesus then ads, *"Therefore be on alert, for you do not know which day your Lord is coming"* (Matt. 24:42). The Lord issues the command to be ready because he intends to separate some believers from others through a special rapture. When God removes the first fruits, this becomes the warning to everyone else that there will be the removal of people from the Earth in the future.

Can you imagine laying in your bed and all of the sudden your spouse disappears? Can you imagine two people driving in a car on the highway one disappears and the other remains? The reality of some believers disappearing while others remain on the Earth will cause sheer chaos and terror.

Revelation chapter 12 verse 5 also sheds light on this issue. *"And she gave birth to a son, a male child, who is to rule all the nations with a rod of iron; and her child was caught up to God and to His throne."* This is the removal of the first fruits that happens before the tribulation. If you continue reading the Scripture, after the "male child" was caught up, the woman fled into the wilderness and was there for 1260 days. This is the time of the tribulation. This verse coincides with Revelation chapter 2 verses 26 and 27. The "male child" represents the overcoming believers whom God will not allow to experience any part of the tribulation.

Another reason I believe speaks of the removal of the first fruits from the Earth is because they are caught up to the throne of God, whereas the general removal of believers are raptured to the air (1 Thes. 4:17). They do not make it to the throne. They did not attain to the same heavenly position that those in Revelation chapter 12 attained.

Another distinguishing characteristic is that the angel blows trumpet before removing the people in First Thessalonians chapter 4. However, no trumpet sounds for the overcomers/ first fruits. Jesus catches them away like a thief in the night. The only way you attain to this first removal is that you are faithful and watchful; otherwise, the trumpet blows because people have no sense of what is getting ready to happen.

Finally, there is a promise to the overcoming believers in

the church of Philadelphia that the Lord will not allow them to go through the "hour of testing" which others will endure (Rev. 3:10). The great tribulation will test the character and patience of all who live upon the Earth. Since the overcomers in the church of Philadelphia have proven themselves already, they do not need to be tried again.

The General Resurrection of the Church

When will the rapture and resurrection of the Church take place? I believe it will happen before God pours out His wrath upon the Earth. The Bible clearly states that when God redeemed us, we escape His wrath; instead, we obtain salvation (1 Thes. 5:9).

The wrath of God occurs during the sounding of the last trumpet, also known as the "seventh trumpet" (Rev. 6:12-17; 14:18-20). There are two aspects coordinated with the blowing of this trumpet – negative and positive. There is the negative side containing the last "woe" of the seven (Rev. 15:1-16:21). The positive aspect includes the general harvesting of the church, the judgement of the saints occurs and Christ begins his 1000 years of reigning (Rev. 11:15-17, 19:7-19).

Chapter seven of the book of Revelation shows that God seals 144,000 from the tribes of Israel. Following this sealing, events begin to take place that usher in the wrath of God. A further look in chapter fourteen of Revelation shows the actual removing of the church from the Earth before the initiation of God's wrath. Those of the church who are not overcomers or first fruits will endure at least a part of the tribulation which consists of the wrath of the devil (Dan. 7:25; Rev. 13:6-9). First Thessalonians 4:15-17 and Revelation 14:15, 16 are two more passages that give us more information about this removal.

First Thessalonians chapter 4 shows us the second advent of Christ. He returns from heaven in preparation for the concluding judgements then establishes his kingdom. If we look observably at this scripture, we will notice several things about the process of the general harvesting of the church: (A) This is the first phase of Christ's second coming (the invisible aspect). (B) The church is raptured into the air to meet the Lord in the clouds (he has not made it to the Earth yet). (C) The dead proceed the saints who are alive coming into the presence of Christ. The book of Revelation adds further detail as to the timing of this event.

In Revelation chapter 14, the reaping or harvesting of the church takes place prior to the gathering of the "clusters from the vine of the Earth" which is the gathering of the unbelievers who will undergo the wrath of God (Isa. 63:1-6; Rev. 14:18-20). The battle of Armageddon is alluded to here, which is the initiation of God's wrath. This means there is a complete removal of the church from the Earth prior to the battle of Armageddon, which is at the conclusion of the tribulation. Therefore, the church in general will experience at least some of the tribulation because that consists of the "wrath of the devil" not the "wrath of God" (Dan. 7:25; Matt. 24:29-31; Rev. 12:6, 17).

The Resurrection of Israel

We can understand the resurrection concerning Israel as we observe several passages of scripture (Isa. 26:19; Ezek. 37:7-17; Dan. 12:1-3). From these portions of the Bible, we have a bird's eye view of the resurrection of Israel and their massive migration back to their land at the dawning of the millennial reign of Christ.

During the great tribulation, Israel will become the object of the Antichrist's wrath (Jer. 30:4-9; Matt. 24:15-22; Rev. 13:7). The archangel Michael shall become their protector, and only those whose names are written in the "book" will live through this time of great trouble while others are killed by the Antichrist (Dan. 12:1). After the time of tribulation, those who have died during the ages gone by along with those who were killed during the Antichrist's wrath will be raised to live on Earth during the millennium with bodies of flesh and blood (Dan. 12:2).

These bodies are typified in the book of Ezekiel where he describes a valley full of "dry bones" (Ezek. 37:1-14).

The bodies in the valley were dead men of Israel that God restored to life, through the prophetic words of Ezekiel, **with** bodies of flesh and blood, **not** spiritual bodies like the church will have. Following this resurrection, there will be a mass migration of the Israelites back into their land (Isa. 27:12, 13; Jer. 23:8; Ezek. 37:12; Zech. 10:10-12).

Israel will neither be raptured to the throne of God nor the clouds. They will not have spiritual bodies. They will have bodies of flesh and live on Earth. Out of all the references to the national restoration and resurrection of Israel, none gives any indication to Israel having spiritual bodies. They all show that the people of Israel have fleshly bodies when they enter the millennium (Isa 65:20-23).

The Resurrection of the Tribulation Saints

These people represent the gleanings of Leviticus. In Revelation chapter twenty, we see preparations made for Christ's millennium reign to begin. An angel binds Satan, casting him into a bottomless pit for one thousand years. His influence upon the nations will be non-existent during the reign of Christ.

In verse four there are two groups of people mentioned. The first are the Christian overcomers whom the Lord gives seats from which they will assist him in the administration of his government. *"Then I saw thrones, and they sat on them, and judgement was given to them…"* (Rev. 20:4) It will become their responsibility to execute the business of judgement over the masses (Luke 19:17, 18; Rev. 2:26, 27).

The next segment of this verse deals with a different group of people. *"…and I saw the souls of those who had been beheaded because of their testimony of Jesus and because of the word of God, and those who had not worshiped the beast or his image, and had not received the mark on their forehead and on their hand; and they came to life and reigned with Christ for a thousand years"* (Rev. 20:4b).

God desires so much for people to reign with Christ that He is willing to give people opportunity even during the tribulation to obtain this goal. However, the price to reign with Christ will be much greater.

To qualify as overcomers now, we must merely deny ourselves, abstaining from worldly lust and be a committed follower of Jesus Christ. The price for being an overcomer during the tribulations is physical death.

During the perils of the tribulation, anyone who does not receive the mark of the beast or his image will be executed (Rev. 13:15). Yet, as a result of their faithfulness during these times of distress and hardship, Christ raises them to reign with him during the thousand years.

Although they reign with Christ, there is no mention of them having thrones and the ability to make judicial decisions like the overcomers of the church. They will not have the benefits or blessings that the overcomers in the church receive (Rev. 7:13-15).

The Resurrection of the Millennial Saints

There will be a need to resurrect individuals who died during the reign of Christ. As mentioned earlier, those who live on the Earth during the thousand years will have physical bodies of flesh and blood. They will procreate, build houses and do things that people do with fleshly bodies. Since they have material bodies, they will still be subject to death and decay (Isa. 65:17-25, 66:22, 23). Death will not be completely defeated until the Lord deals with it at the great white throne (Rev. 20:14).

The citizens of the millennial kingdom will include Israel as well as Gentile nations. Some of these individuals are converted while others will remain obstinate, merely giving an external display of obedience. This is why at the end of these thousand years Satan shall be loosed and can deceive the nations once more, showing the sin element will still exist during the millennium (Isa. 65:20; Rev. 20:7, 8). The deceived people are the ones who never completely submitted to Christ. Remember, some individuals of the nations will have to be beat into subjection (Rev. 2:26, 27).

When the angel releases Satan, he will be able to deceive those who were rebels at heart. There will be one final great battle between Christ and Satan called Gog and Magog (Rev. 20:7, 8). After this, the Lord casts him into the lake of fire. Then there is the appearance of a great white throne (Rev. 20:10, 11). It is from here that the Lord executes the last judgements concerning those who died in the millennium, the unsaved, the rebellious angels and demons.

When the Lord raises the believers who died during the

millennium, this becomes the conclusion of the first order of the resurrection (Rev. 20:6). The resurrection of the millennial saints can be observed in Revelation 20:12, *"And I saw the dead, the great and the small, standing before the throne, and books were opened; and another book was opened, which is the book of life; and the dead were judged from the things which were written in the books, according to their deeds."*

Notice in verse twelve the word "dead". This should be understood as the rest of the dead. This would include those who died in the millennium (righteous and unrighteous) as well as the unsaved throughout all the history of time. As such, this verse cannot be limited to the judgement of the wicked only.

Since every person of every generation throughout time must stand before Christ to be judged, this must also include those from the millennium (Rom. 10:14; 2 Cor. 5:10).

From studying the rapture and resurrection, we see that this period of resurrecting people is going to take a process of years. It will begin with the rapture of the Church and conclude at the great white throne.

The Raising of the Fallen Angels and Demons

These eternal beings are comprised of those who cohabitated with Earthly women creating giants in the Earth, those who rebelled with Satan and the beings which became demons (Gen. 6:2; Matt. 12:43; Rev. 12:7-9).

The Bible records this phrase, *"And the sea gave up the dead which were in it..."* (Rev. 20:13a). This statement cannot be referring to unsaved people since all of the unbelievers who die whether by sea, disease etc. are in Hades or hell. Many think this phrase refers to the sea releasing all demons (Matt. 8:31, 32).

G. H. Pember wrote a book entitled *Earth's Earliest Ages*. In it he discusses how there were beings during the original creation of the Earth that followed Satan and his angels in rebellion against God. When God judged Satan, the rebellious angels and these beings, some of them (the beings) became disembodied spirits called demons. Their judgement was supposedly confinement by the depths of the waters. Other people, such as Witness Lee, also believe the depths of the water became the lodging place of demons after their judgement.

As it pertains to the angels who facilitated the commingling of the angelic beings with the human race, God put them in chains under darkness in *Tartarus* (the deepest darkest part of Hades) until they are brought forth in the coming day of judgement – the "great day" (2 Pet. 2:4; Jude 1:6).

The phrase "great day" refers to the final day of judgement. For these rebellious angels and demons, this will be at the great white throne. These angels will suffer the greatest eternal punishment.

One final thought about the "sea" (Rev. 20:13a). It is interesting to note that when Christ has finished his judgement of the angels, the Earth and its inhabitants, we find in chapter twenty-one that there will be no more "sea" when the new heaven and new Earth are revealed.

Why is there no more sea? Since God created the seas as a place of judgement for demons, once God releases them for judgement, He does not need this prison. (Gen. 1:9-10; Jer. 5:22). This means that God has finished judging demons. There will however, be fresh water upon the new

Earth. There is only the elimination of seas such as the Mediterranean, Aegean and Black seas.

The Resurrection of the Unsaved

Finally, there will be the resurrection of the unsaved who partake of the second resurrection or the resurrection of judgement (John 5:29). *"...and death and Hades gave up the dead which were in them..."* (Rev. 20:13). No doubt, some of these unrepentant individuals have had graves of water whether through drowning or the ashes of the dead being release into the sea as a farewell. However, these are all concluded to be in the temporary holding place of hell or Hades.

This resurrection and judgement of the unsaved, rebellious angels and demons will occur after the millennium resulting with them being thrown into the lake of fire (John 5:28, 29; 1 Cor. 15:23, 24; Rev. 20:15).

THE SOWING OF BARE GRAIN

"But someone will say, 'How are the dead raised? And with what kind of body do they come?' You fool! That which you sow does not come to life unless it dies; and that which you sow, you do not sow the body which used to be, but bare grain, perhaps of wheat or of something else. But God gives it a body just as He wished, and to each of the seeds a body of its own" (1 Cor. 15:35-38)

Jesus also spoke of this bare grain when he said, *Truly, truly I say to you, unless a grain of wheat falls into the earth and dies, it remains alone; but if it dies, it bears much fruit"* (John 12:24). These two passages of Scripture show exactly what you are planting. You are not sowing your body as a seed, rather your soul. The bare grain is the soul separated from the body.

As you read further in the gospel of John, Jesus' next words are recorded. *"He who loves his life loses it, and he who hates his life in this world will keep it to eternal life"* (John 12:25). The issue that Jesus was dealing with was the sowing of his soul life in order that we may have eternal life. Then he shows us that we must do the same. Our souls become the bare grain that we sow. The way you plant your soul determines how your new body will look.

The true goal of First Corinthians 15 is not a new body. That will be given to everyone. Rather, the emphasis is the planting of the soul life. How your body will look is automatically determined by how you seeded your soul.

As you look at Jesus's words again, the planting of the soul is really a death process. It is not allowing your soul to participate in the lust of this world; instead, you take up your cross daily and follow the path of Jesus. You sow grain but God gives the body based upon how well you sow your soul (1 Cor. 15:38).

The reward of your sowing is a glorified body (1 Cor. 15:39-42). Accordingly, each person's body will look different because of how they planted their soul.

Paul wrote that stars have different levels of shining. He also said the glory of the moon is different from the glory of the sun. He writes that this is how the resurrection will be (1 Cor. 15:39-42). How you will look in the future is based upon how well you planted bare grain (soul).

THE VIRTUES OF THE RESURRECTION BODY

There are two types of bodies given when the resurrection occurs. Some will have bodies of flesh and blood. Israel and every other nation living on Earth during the millennium will possess this type of body. The other, spiritual bodies will be given to the church. Our bodies will consist of flesh and bone enlivened by the Spirit (Luke 24:39).

Paul gives his insights concerning what he believes the resurrection body will be like for the church. He states that it will be incorruptible, glorious, powerful and spiritual.

An incorruptible body means that it will not be subject to the diseases that currently plague the human body. Neither will we die. There will be no decaying of these bodies since the word "incorruptible" shows the absence of sin (1 Cor. 15:42).

When Adam rebelled against God, sin entered the body and death because of it. This means that at the point of his defiance, humankind became subject to the sicknesses and diseases that would eventually plague humanity. When we are raised, God gives us a body absent of sin; consequently, not subject to decay.

This body will also be glorious compared to the natural body we have now (1 Cor. 15:43). In comparison to our new body, this physical body is dishonorable. Why does Paul say this if God created man in his image? Again, it is because sin corrupted the body. In addition to diseases, there are also people who are born disfigured. This is all the result of sin. To deal with this issue, God will beautify us with glory.

Another trait of this body is that it possesses great power (1 Cor. 15:43). Today, as we grow older in age, our bodies become weaker in strength. However, these new bodies will always have the power to do what God intends for us to do. We will never grow tired and need to rest. Our bodies will have an unending strength in which we can forever experience the fullness of eternity with God.

The apostle Paul also says that our bodies will be spiritual (1 Cor. 15:44). "Spiritual" here does not mean that it is not physical. It indicates that our future body will be under the control of our soul, which will be a complete compliance to the will of the Spirit. During this age, we must fight to overcome the sinful desires of the flesh; however, after the resurrection, our bodies will be under the total control of a pure soul. Your new body will not be subject to fleshly desires any longer.

Since your body will be similar to Jesus', you will be able to teleport yourself from one place to another. This is also an aspect of being a spiritual body. On one occasion, the disciples were cowering in a room behind a locked door. Instead of Jesus knocking on the door, he simply appeared in the room (Luke 24:36; John 20:19).

Jesus was also able to change his external appearance (Mark 16:12). This is why the disciples did not recognize him (Luke 24:16). I do not know if there will be a need for us to alter our appearance in the future. However, this shows the greatness of the new bodies we will receive. What the Bible shows us about the resurrection body is that we will be freed from any restraints that have been placed on us by the material body we presently have.

HINTS OF AN OUT-RESURRECTION

Paul writes a statement in Philippians which states, *"In order that I may attain to the resurrection from the dead"* (Philip. 3:11). This statement could contain some evidence of a special resurrection for those whose lives are most precious to God. This is dubbed by some as an "out-resurrection" or "extra-resurrection".

This topic is one of much controversy. Some believe that this statement pertains to the general resurrection from the dead in which all believers will participate while others believe this speaks of a very distinct resurrection (an outstanding one) that separates the overcoming believers from all other believers. This one passage reveals God's great intention for those believers who choose to overcome instead of being overcome by sin, the flesh or the Devil.

The certainty of the resurrection is found throughout the entire Bible. It seems here however, that Paul was not sure if he was going to be included in this particular resurrection. Why does he possibly introduce doubt if the resurrection will occur for everyone (Acts 24:15; 1 Thes. 4:15-17)?

The word resurrection is a special one here. Normally, it is rendered *anastasis* in the Greek. This is the only instance in the Bible where it is rendered *exanastasis*. The preface "ex" means "out" or "from". The world should literally be understood as "out-resurrection", "outstanding resurrection" or "extra-resurrection." This is not the same as the general resurrection, which everyone will experience.

There are differences of opinion as to what this word really means. Some believe that it merely speaks of the resurrection of the just in contrast to the unjust. But to be a part of this resurrection, Paul gave his most intense effort to participate with Christ in every aspect possible here and now. He was not indicating that all of his life was spent just to make the resurrection of the just because all believers no matter how they lived will be a part of this resurrection (2 Cor. 5:10).

In verse twelve thru fourteen Paul further adds, *"Not that I have already obtained it or have already become perfect, but I press on so that I may lay hold of that for which also I was laid hold of by Christ Jesus. Brethren, I do not regard myself as having laid hold of it yet; but one thing I do: forgetting what lies behind and reaching forward to what lies ahead, I press on toward the goal for the prize of the upward call of God in Christ Jesus"* (Philip. 3:12-14).

Observe this text carefully. Paul considered this resurrection as a prize to be obtained by the one whose character has been thoroughly dealt with. Nowhere else in the Bible is the resurrection considered to be a prize. Here, however, the apostle presents it as something to be won.

G. H. Lang interprets this resurrection as a special one for believers who have made themselves "worthy". By worthy he means that you have worked for and earned this reward. Only the saints who separate themselves from the status quo will be ready to receive this great prize. However, this resurrection is a prize that God will allow every overcoming believer to partake of.

Before and after Paul makes this great statement concerning the resurrection, he declares that there are things which he is doing to ensure that he can participate in this resurrection (Philip. 3:10, 12). These elements, along with the structure of the statement about the resurrection, give occasion for us to reason if there is a special resurrection to which Paul is referring.

In verse ten, he states, *"That I may know Him and the power of His resurrection and the fellowship of His sufferings, being conformed to His death..."* This verse ends with a semicolon and continues with his statement about the resurrection as if the elements in verse ten must occur in order for him to partake of the resurrection.

The first segment of this verse contains the words "know him". This is an experience, not mere intellectual ascendancy. Paul's desire was to become intimately associated with Christ in order to be thoroughly infused and saturated with his nature.

This begins with salvation and continues with daily fellowship with Jesus Christ. You cannot be partaker of this special resurrection without "knowing him". In fact, if he does not truly know you, he will make this statement to you, "I never knew you, depart from me." (Matt. 7:23)

The next element is "the power of his resurrection." Notice the word "and" between these two phrases. To know Christ was one thing. To experience the power of his resurrection is another. You should understand this as the power, that which proceeds from the resurrection. If God raised Jesus from the dead then He can, by this same power, instruct, reform and redefine your character.

Paul was interested in an inner change. It was not enough for him to be saved. He wanted to undergo a complete change inwardly. Without this change, there was no guarantee of him participating in this special resurrection.

The third aspect here is the "fellowship of his sufferings". Enduring suffering enables you to become intricately tied to the ultimate experience of Christ – his death. Enduring suffering ensures that you become a joint-heir with Christ when he is manifested in his complete glory (Rom. 8:17; 1 Pet. 1:7).

It is from this experience that Paul makes the statement "in order that". Verse ten was the way to obtain the resurrection of verse eleven. This phrase can imply two things. The first is uncertainty. The second is an emphatic assertion that he is doing whatever it takes to partake of this resurrection.

This special resurrection will take place at the judgement seat of Christ after the initial resurrection and judgement of the saints. The pursuit of this prize should be your life-long goal. In fact, Paul says that every believer should conduct his or her life in pursuit of this "high calling" (Phil. 3:15).

In order for Paul to obtain this "extra-resurrection" he had to forget about the things that were in his past – accomplishments as well as failures; instead, he reached forward to what lay in front of him. In fact, this unique resurrection was so important to Paul that he decided, no matter what he was experiencing in life, he would press his way forward.

The apostle concludes his discussion by indicating that the more mature believers should think the same way in pursuing the prize of the out-resurrection. If anyone does not think this way, *"God will reveal that also to you"* (Phil. 3:15).

Your life should be so focused on the out-resurrection that you will not allow anything to distract you. Do not allow your successes or failures to become a distraction. Forget everything and pursue the one thing – the out-resurrection.

ETERNAL JUDGEMENT

What you believe about the future will affect how you live today. In the opening scene of the sizzling movie Gladiator, General Maximus Decimus Meridius (Russell Crowe) gives a motivational speech to his valiant soldiers. Seated on his horse, facing those under his command, he says to them, "Brothers, what we do in life echoes in eternity." With these words, those warriors, in the face of fear, certain bloodshed and even death for some, marched into battle on behalf of the Roman Empire. That phrase holds more truth than we know. What you do now will be apparent in eternity. All that you do in life presently will follow you into judgement and eternity.

Understanding eternal judgement will perhaps give you the greatest appreciation for what God is doing throughout the ages. Judgement reverberates throughout the Bible from Genesis to Revelation. Sometimes God would judge a nation. Other times He judges the individual. Judgement is an essential part of life to keep us in the way of righteousness as well as give us an expectation for what will occur in the future.

When you consider future judgement, you must not attach purely a negative connotation to it. It is not merely for dealing out retribution or punishment. There is a greater emphasis of rewarding those who are faithful and obedient (2 Cor. 5:10). Through the coming judgements, particularly of believers, God will distinguish those who were most loyal to Him from the pretenders.

Considering the judgement of God should give you a healthy fear of what you will experience if you do not live a life pleasing to God. It also gives you a joyous expectation because God intends to reward His faithful servants (Heb. 11:6). Therefore, it behoves us to understand how God intends to deal with humanity and the church. Keep this in mind. God's judgements are always right because He judges according to truth.

The phrase "eternal judgement" speaks clearly and definitively about the final judgements. They are His final ones and are eternal in nature. They are non-reversible and non-negotiable. Some of these are progressive, such as the sentencing of Satan, the angels and sin. The remaining eternal decrees pertain strictly to the future, around the time of the initiation of the millennial reign of Christ. These consist of the judgement seat of Christ, the judgement of the nations, judgement of the Antichrist and false prophet, the great white throne judgement and the judgement of the Earth.

Let us take a brief look at the words "eternal" and "judgement". The word eternal refers to something existing throughout all the ages; consequently, what God sets in motion through eternal judgement will be irreversible.

The word judgement has many connotations to it. One definition refers to administering justice. This was done by the king in the Old Testament. He would take care of any issues deriving from conflict. It also speaks of investigating or scrutinizing an issue and rendering a verdict. This is the focus of eternal judgement.

The rendering of a ruling or decree places emphasis upon the Judge primarily. However, as consequence of the sentence passed, there is also an obligation placed upon those who have been favorably judged. Those among men who have shown themselves faithful in following Christ will successfully pass through judgement and be given authority to assist in administering Christ's governmental rule (Rev. 2:26, 27).

The word "scrutinize" holds primary importance. These final judgements are primarily for the purpose of examination of works. Future judgement is not about deciding who is saved and who is not. This has already been determined by the group you are being presently judged with. If you are at the judgement seat of Christ, you are a part of the body of Christ. With the exception of those who came from the millennium, if you appear at the great white throne, you are not saved.

In Ecclesiastes, there is a verse that has a particular relevance for our study. In chapter twelve, verses thirteen and fourteen we are told of the responsibility that has been placed upon mankind, *"The conclusion, when all has been heard, is: fear God and keep His commandments, because this applies to every person. For God shall bring every act to judgement, everything which is hidden, whether it is good, or evil."* Our sole responsibility is to revere God and obey His decrees because at the end of the day, God is going to bring every act into judgement whether it is seen or unseen, good or evil. Whatever transpires in your life, God will bring it into judgement. Nothing you do escapes the attention of God.

Others may not know your faults, secrets or hidden agendas, but God will shed light upon these when judgement occurs. Some people think that because their family and friends do not see the bad things they do, that they are okay.

Paul tells Timothy that some people's sins are manifest now whereas others are kept secret and are only revealed at the judgement seat of Christ (1 Tim. 5:24). For instance, some people engage in extramarital affairs and no one ever finds out. This sin will meet the person at judgement.

Some people have a problem with God because they believe He sits back and allows so many bad things to happen to the innocent and good people. They reason, if God is so good, why He permits murder, rape and the sexual assault of children and the elderly. Well, this is the purpose of future judgement.

In the future judgement, God is going to deal with every sin and atrocity that people thought He was allowing to happen without any retribution. God will show every man, woman and child who is at the age of accountability what He thinks about the acts they have committed.

We must base everything we do in life upon the fact that we are subject to the authority of God. We obey Him because we recognize His supremacy. He is infinite and we are finite. He has created the world and everything in it. As we submit to His complete rule in this life, we guarantee our success in the coming time of examination of our works. God will show everyone what He thinks of his or her life at the judgement. For some people it will be a time of rejoicing. For others, it will be a time of sheer terror.

THERE MUST BE JUDGEMENT

Through judgement, God shows justice and highlights His righteousness. God's reveals His righteous character in rewarding the faithful and judging the disobedient (Heb. 11:6). So, there must be judgement to eliminate sin and to completely vindicate God's righteousness and character. After all the evil deeds and disobedience have seemingly eclipsed the reality of God's existence, eternal judgement will show who He is and what He stands for.

If God does not judge sin, He will never visibly prove to the world that He is a holy God because there will remain the apparent persistence of sin in the Earth which is the source of all antagonistic thoughts and actions towards Him. Because of His holiness, God cannot be tied to sin; therefore, He must pronounce judgement upon sin and sinners.

The certainty of future judgement creates a healthy "fear of the Lord". Paul writes a statement to the Corinthians, which reflects his attitude towards future judgement. He writes, *"Knowing the fear of the Lord, we persuade men..."* (2 Cor. 5:11a). The apostle makes it clear that the coming judgement will reveal the good and bad things that one has done with their body (2 Cor. 5:10). If you are persuaded of the possible terrors of the future judgements, you should not only discipline your life but also plead with others to become Christians and live productive lives (Matt. 25:24).

THE JUDGE

Scripture makes it clear that God is the Supreme judge (Ps. 96:11-13; Heb. 12:23). However, we are also told that God has committed all judgement to Christ who will become the just judge of everyone and everything examining all evidence, and will make his verdicts based upon the standards of righteousness and the Word (John 5:22; Acts 10:42, 17:31). These judgements will consist of both reward and punishment.

Christ's place of ruling is seen as a courtroom. This will

not be an unfamiliar scenario. In the Old Testament, those who were judges sat upon a high seat (Ex. 18:13). One of the duties of the Roman governor was to sit as a judge.

In addition to these examples, we are innovated with court shows on television. There is even a program called Street Court. Instead of the judge sitting in a formal courtroom, he addresses each case in the different locations where the problem has occurred. His place of ruling moves from place to place.

In whatever setting the judge is in, it is their responsibility to determine the guilt or innocence of a person, as well as what sentence was to should be given. This was the case in the Old Testament. The judge would set his seat up in any given location and perform his duties.

Christ's judgement seat will also be mobile. Initially it will be in the air where he will judge the Church (1 Cor. 3:11f; 1 Thes. 4:15f). From there, his throne will be located in Jerusalem (Micah 4:1-3). This will be the place where his rule will issue from during the millennium. Finally, he will sit upon a great white throne (Rev. 20:11). Although we are not told where this throne will be located, it is clear that Christ's seat of judgement will move from place to place.

This throne is symbolic of Christ's kingly and judicial powers (Isa. 9:7; 1 Tim. 6:15). He will become the visible king of the whole Earth (Dan. 2:44). As king, he will righteously judge all.

WORKS ANALYZED

All the judgements of Christ upon people or nations is based upon their works (Matt. 25; 1 Cor. 3:12-15; Rev. 20:12). The message was given to the seven churches of Asia

Minor was "I know thy works" (Rev. 2:1-2). Every reward or act of discipline is and will be based upon what an individual has done with their life (2 Cor. 5:10). In essence, you have some part in determining what God is going to decide about your life. He makes the decree, but you present Him with the facts based upon how you live your life presently.

There are three areas of your life that will come under intense scrutiny by Jesus Christ. He will examine your actions, thoughts and words (Matt. 12:36; 37; Luke 19:15-27; Rom. 2:15, 16; 1 Cor. 3:12f). These three groups comprise our "works". This is a sobering reality. Nothing that happens in your life that will escape examination (Ps.62:12b).

Actions are the most obvious area that will be inspected. Most people who understand judgement are conscious of this. Many believe that righteous living will guarantee their entrance into heaven while those who lived sinful lives will go to hell. This is by far the most popular view held of the coming judgements.

I do agree that our works will play a significant role in the degree of what we receive and how we operate in the future (Rev. 22:12). What I disagree with is the opinion that one's righteousness or sin will determine if he or she will go to heaven or hell. I repeat, the future judgements are not about determining where one's future destiny will be. That is already decided by where you are standing in judgement.

No, these judgements are to determine what type of reward or punishment you will be given because of the life you have lived. In other words, one who is saved will spend eternity with God, but Christ's examination of the believer will determine exactly how much of the blessedness he or she will experience (Matt. 25:21).

Similarly, the unredeemed will spend eternity in the lake of fire, but Christ judges them to determine how much of hell they will experience (Matt. 10:15, 11:20-24). Many of the passages of Scripture that deal with future judgement pertains to a person's actions as the basis for their success of failure when Christ returns (Matt. 16:27; 1 Cor. 3:14).

Another area of a person's life that will be under scrutiny is their thoughts (Rom. 2:14, 15). In Romans chapter two, we are given the picture of a judgement scene. There will be a trial, with the witness being the thoughts of a man. Some thoughts may assume the role of prosecuting attorney while others will represent the defense. They will be the cause of either this person's guilt or acquittal.

Whether or not an individual has had a track passed out to them or heard a televangelist preach is of little consequence. Judgement must proceed because God has allowed man's conscience to direct him morally. Righteousness must become the fruit of every person's life. The conscience allows every person to know what God concludes to be proper conduct and what will be condemned.

The word "secrets" in Romans 2:16 also pertains to a man's feelings and desires. These will also be judged. Every aspect of man will come under the scrutiny of Jesus Christ. Every evil desire or unrighteous feeling will be severely dealt with (Matt. 5:27, 28).

Finally, every idle word will be judged (Matt. 12:36). Does this mean that we must only talk about spiritual things? The meaning of the statement in Matthew pertains to speaking hurtful things. Words that people speak to damage other's integrity, relationships emotional stability etc. These are words spoken with the intent of being malicious. Our words must only be those that minister grace into an individual's life (Eph. 4:29).

If we know that the total man will be judge at "the day", then we would be wise to prepare ourselves completely. If we judge ourselves daily, inspecting our works (deeds, thoughts and words), we are guaranteed to have confidence at his coming.

The only reason you will fail is that you have a limited comprehension about what will take place in the future. A reason for this is because it is difficult to place value on what God is offering in eternity. Although we preach about it, we have not been there, so there remains some uncertainty about it.

If you know someone who won a $50 million dollar lottery, you will begin to see his or her life change. They will probably buy a bigger house, new cars, new clothes and maybe some jewellery. You see the results of their new wealth and it may perhaps inspire you to play the lottery.

However, it is difficult to place value upon the significant results for those Christ deemed faithful at the judgement, because no one has ever experienced them yet. Therefore, the immature in Christ find it difficult to stay focused on what lies in the future. If what lies in the future is not important enough to you, there will be little discipline in your life.

THE DAY

The eternal judgements will all be put into effect during what the Bible terms "the day". "The day" speaks of

Christ's second coming; consequently, it always points to future events. Christ's return initiates the beginning of "the day". It will conclude with the great white throne judgement. Therefore, "the day" deals with the complete time span of future judgements beginning with the judgement seat of Christ and concluding with the great white throne judgement (2 Tim. 4:1).

This time will be characterized by famine, the Earth undergoing cataclysmic events and extreme darkness (Joel 2:1-11; Rev. 6:12-13). Men and women will finally endure the sentence imposed upon them by the righteous judge (Luke 21:25, 26). Since it will encompass all the final judgements, "the day" will last at least 1000 years (2 Pet. 3:8).

THE JUDGEMENTS

The Judgement of Satan

This was the first judgement to take place that had eternal consequences. The judgement of Satan is different from that of humankind. Due to the infusion of sin into the human nature, we can be recovered. However, Satan - along with the angels who revolted with him - can never be restored because of who he (an angel) was as well as the location of his rebellion – heaven. In fact, Jesus says that the lake of fire was created for the devil and those who followed him in the uprising (Matt. 25:41). His destiny is forever determined.

There are two kings referred to in the prophetical books which many believe are the parallel of Satan. Some would say these are literal kings and do not refer to Satan. However, according to Hebrew writings, Jews understood that sometimes human events represented what occurred in

Heaven. Therefore, the language could change to reflect this. I would like to present these next passages of two kings as being analogous to Satan.

The first person is the king of Babylon as recorded in Isaiah chapter fourteen. The prophet Isaiah is giving Israel a word concerning their recovery from bondage to the Babylonians. Within this prophetic word, the king of Babylon is more directly addressed (Isa. 14:4). It is between verses twelve and seventeen that many believe is a description of the judgement of Satan.

In verse twelve, we see him referred to as "Lucifer" which means morning star. The Bible also refers to him as "star of the morning". As part of Satan's prominence, there was some type of light that emanated from him. Second Corinthians states that Satan can "disguise himself as an angel of light" (2 Cor. 11:14).

Even though he has been judged, he has not lost his ability to express the same light, which manifests in the heavenly angels. Jesus Christ though, is the bearer of the greatest light – the glory of God (John 1:7-9, 14; Rev. 21:23, 24). Isaiah proceeds next to tell why Satan fell.

There are five reasons, all beginning with "I will". "I will ascend into heaven," "I will raise my throne above the stars of God" (the angels are sometimes referred to as stars Job 38:7), "I will sit on the mount of assembly in the recesses of the north", "I will ascend above the heights of the clouds" and "I will make myself like the Most High."

The ultimate goal of Lucifer was to be like God (Isa. 14:14). God's reaction to the Devil's revolt was so swift that Jesus described his descent from heaven as lightening (Luke 10:18).

The king of Tyrus was the second person whose impending judgement is seen as the antitype of Satan being judged. In Ezekiel, we have more descriptive words as to the physical appearance of Satan (Ezek. 28:12-19). From these verses, it can be clearly seen that there was none created like "Lucifer".

The first words spoken against him were, *"You had the seal of perfection, Full of wisdom and perfect in beauty"* (Ezek. 28:12). Some believe this is God speaking about Satan being created in a state of perfection. Others believe this statement reflects what Satan thought about himself. Whichever you believe to be true, one thing is for sure, he was full of wisdom and perfectly beautiful. The acknowledgment of his beauty and wisdom were the first signs of his sin of pride (Prov. 6:16, 16:18, 21:4).

"You were in Eden, the garden of God..." (Ezek. 28:13).This could point to the fact that he had responsibility in the Garden of Eden before Adam. Therefore, it would make sense that he instigated this atrocity in the garden because Adam was put there in his place.

As we read further we are told of precious stones that became the covering for Lucifer. *"...Every precious stone was your covering: The ruby, the topaz, and the diamond; The beryl, the onyx and the jasper; the lapis lazuli, the turquoise and the emerald; And the gold..."* (Ezek. 28:13). This could mean that they were present as a part of the garden which became his covering as he remained in it. It could also mean that these magnificent stones were a part of his appearance. Therefore, he could be called the "star of the morning" indicating that there was brilliance to his expression.

Along with these stones, there is the mention of tabrets (tambourines) and pipes that were "in him". This could possibly mean that as he went from place to place there was a sound of music emanating from his being. His every act of motion was perpetual praise and worship to God (Ezek. 28:13).

He was also the *"anointed cherub who covers..."* (Ezek. 28:14). Although we are looking at the judgement of Satan via the judgement of the king of Tyrus, this statement is rarely applied to people. The word cherub refers to a certain class of angels whose job was to cover. The cherubim that covered the mercy seat upon the ark depict this covering (Ex. 25:17-22).

The book of Hebrews addresses this issue of covering. In chapter nine verse 5 the Bible shows us a greater revelation of Cherubim. The scripture proclaims they are, *"The cherubim of glory overshadowing the mercy seat"* (Heb. 9:5). The assignments of these angels are to promote and protect the glory of God and as such are among the highest-ranking angels. Lucifer, as a cherub was created for this job (Ezek. 10:4). No one had a greater rank than him.

Ezekiel also states that *"...You were on the holy mountain of God; You walked in the midst of the stones of fire"* (Ezek. 28:14). Both of these statements refer to the divine presence of God (Ps. 15:1, 24:3; Enoch 18:6-11). Satan had an access to God unlike any other of the created beings. In short, he was the most perfectly created being with the most privileges.

Further in the chapter, the prophet pens that *"...unrighteousness was found in you"* (Ezek. 28:15). Every person and angelic being that God creates is given a free will. Satan chose to rebel. Ezekiel reveals the source of his iniquity a couple of verses later. His beauty and brilliance corrupted his perception of himself and God (Ezek. 28:17). This became the source of his pride; consequently, his downfall.

His immediate sentence was removal from the presence of God. His liberties were revoked and his habitation switched. The Devil's domain would now become Earth (Job 1:7; 28:18). Although he can come before God, he can only do so now as an adversary (Job 1:6f, 2:1f; Rev. 12:10).

The next major experience of judgement for Satan is to be placed in chains and thrown into a bottomless pit for 1000 years (Rev. 20:1-3). During the time of the millennial kingdom of Christ, Satan's presence will not be allowed to be a distraction.

After the 1000 years are finished, Satan is released from this prison to lead people of the nations who were never submitted to Christ in their heart, away from the truth with the expressed purpose of gathering them together for war against Christ Jesus.

Those in his army are destroyed by fire while he finally ends up being cast into the lake of fire. This is the concluding aspect of God's judgement of Satan (Rev. 20:7-10).

The Judgement of the Angels

The angels in view here are those who have fallen from their original positions with God. These fallen angels can also be subdivided into two categories: Those who followed Satan in his rebellion, and those who materialized into fleshly bodies without the approval of God (Gen. 6:1, 2; Rev. 12:3, 4).

I am uncertain as to whether this last group followed Satan in his rebellion and continued to descend in their desires or they simply left their positions with God and materialized in flesh.

The judgement of God upon both classes of these angels

is progressive. The angels who followed Satan in his rebellion were defeated and thrust out of heaven while the angels who materialized in flesh were eventually imprisoned (2 Pet. 2:4; Jude 1:6).

However, their full judgement will be carried out at the great white throne (Isa. 24:21). In the future, the saints will assist Christ in judging these evil angels (1 Cor. 6:3).

The War in Heaven

The war of Satan and his angels against Michael and the righteous angels is recorded in the book of Revelation. In chapter twelve, John has written several verses, which allude to the "great war" in the heavens.

In verse three, we are told that there appeared a great dragon having seven heads, ten horns and seven crowns upon his heads. The literal interpretation of this verse speaks of the antichrist who will assume the kingly role in the future revived Roman Kingdom.

He will have influence over Earthly leaders who will attempt to overcome God's people. However, we can see here the allusion to Satan and the fallen angels. He has influenced a third part of the angels to mutiny against God.

This reference is made even more of a reality for us as we continue to read this chapter. In verses seven thru nine, John mentions the war that was fought between Michael, the loyal angels, Satan and the rebellious angels.

This war did not rage in the heavenly abode of God but among the stars of the universe. There, Satan's rebellion was quelled by Michael. The Dragon along with the wicked angels was cast from their place of residence to the Earth. They would never be allowed to occupy the places of their former habitation.

Although they are the outcast of heaven, God did not bind or cast these angels into prison. They have become the beings that we deal with in everyday life (Eph. 6:12). These angels are presently occupying territories and dominions that have been assigned to them.

For example, an evil spirit vexed Saul (1 Sam. 16:14). The prince of the kingdom of Persia withstood Gabriel when trying to get a message to Daniel from God (Dan. 10:13). Paul had to cast out demons (Acts 16:16-18). Jesus' ministry was all about helping individuals to be freed from evil spirits (Luke 4:18). The battle rages on.

The Angels Who Left Their First Estate

The other group of fallen angels are referred to as "Watchers" or "Grigori." It was their job to watch over the men of the Earth. The book of Enoch says that these angels "kept not their first estate" (Jude 1:6). Genesis describes it this way, *"Now it came about, when men began to multiply on the face of the land, and daughters were born to them, that the sons of God saw that the daughters of men were beautiful; and they took wives for themselves, whomever they chose"* (Gen. 6:1, 2).

The phrase "sons of God" is of special importance. Mentioned only five times in the Old Testament, they all refer to the angels, not humankind (Job. 1:6, 2:1, 38:7).

Enoch records a conversation that he had with God. He tells Enoch that these Watchers left the eternal abode. Instead of dwelling in heaven, they wanted to live in physical bodies to cohabitate with women (Gen 6:1-4; Enoch XV, 2, 3, 6, 7).

The angels who left their "first estate" were even more wicked than those who followed Satan in rebellion since they caused the corruption of the human race. These fallen angels, along with Lucifer and the other rebellious angels can never be restored (Enoch XII. Sect. III, XIV, 4).

According to the book of Enoch, there were about two hundred angels that left heaven. They agreed together with their leader Samyaza that they would all assume equal responsibility for their crime. They had children after marrying the women of the Earth.

The Scripture records the birth of their offspring in Genesis chapter six verse four. They were called "giants" or "Nephilim". These were fallen Earth-born men who had the mixed DNA of the angels and human women.

Their children became so great of stature that there was not enough food to satisfy their hunger. Consequently, they began to feed on the flesh and blood of birds, beasts, reptiles and fish.

The Nephilim are also said to have been the source of evil spirits. Since their union is that of spiritual beings and flesh, they were considered to be evil spirits upon the Earth. Enoch notes that these shall be called "the spirits of the wicked" (Enoch XV, 8).

The book of Enoch further describes the actions of these angels. They also taught the women sorcery, incantations, potions, how to use make-up and how to dye clothes. These fallen angels were the cause of humanity knowing secrets that were never intended to be share.

They eventually altered everything about the world. The thoughts, intentions and DNA make-up of humanity were changed. Humanity was completely changed from the inside out (Gen. 6:5).

The offspring of these angels also had prolonged lives and were endowed with great knowledge because of spiritual secrets revealed to them. All of these elements enabled them to conquer the nations dwelling upon the Earth. This was a crime that God would not allow to go unpunished.

Eventually, God had to destroy all flesh with a flood (Gen. 6:5-7). Humankind as it existed could not be allowed to live upon the Earth. However, even in this God gave them an opportunity to escape judgement. Noah preached but none listened (2 Pet. 2:5). After this the flood came.

Unlike the angels of the rebellion, the initiators of this grievous act were taken, bound with "chains of darkness" and imprisoned within the Earth in a region called Tartarus until the coming judgement of the "great day" (Enoch X, 15).

These are not literal chains. The phrase literally means these angels are confined in the deepest darkest part of Hades (2 Pet. 2:4). Words are not adequate to explain the depth of this term. The book of Jude adds that they are "under darkness" (Jude 1:6). These angels are in the darkest region ever described in Scripture.

The final time of judgement for these fallen angels, evil spirits and demons will be at the great white throne. It is recorded in Revelation, *"And the sea gave up the dead which were in it..."* (Rev. 20:13a).

The book of Enoch states that these fallen angels will be taken away into the lowest pits of the fire where they will be in torment (Enoch X, 16, 17). They will burn with Satan, the Anti-Christ, the False Prophet, the other rebellious angels, demons and the unsaved (Matt. 25:41; Rev. 20:15).

The Judgement of Sin

God must judge sin because He is holy. Sin is what causes us to violate God's laws. This wickedness is the cause of all the evils that are associated with the present state of the world. It is also the very thing that keeps us isolated from any relationship or fellowship with God (John 3:19, 20; Eph. 4:17-20). Such separation is a problem.

God's ultimate goal is to recover every soul. He wants to restore relationship between Himself and us. Therefore, God must deal with every act of sin in order that our relationship with Him can be restored and our fellowship remains unhindered (Heb. 12:5-11).

The judgement of sin began where it first appeared. When Adam disobeyed God's command to abstain from the tree of the knowledge of good and evil, he initiated a process in humanity that would become the cause of our greatest struggle to obey. God began to immediately and swiftly deal with this corruption (Gen. 3:14-19). The serpent, Eve and Adam, were all consequently judged because of their sin.

He dealt with the serpent first because he was the propagator of this tragic deed. God's statement to the serpent was *"...Because you have done this"* (Gen. 3:14). The rebellion in heaven was initiated by Satan. Now he has infected humanity with sin. Here he is judged a second time with God changing the form of the serpent.

The serpent would become the most detestable of all creatures. His mobility would be reduced to the ground. This would become the symbol that he was to be considered the lowest and most detestable of all creatures.

In addition, the great Redeemer, Jesus Christ, who would "bruise his head", would eventually destroy him. This statement has reference to the re-establishing of authority to humankind.

The woman would be made to experience indescribable pain when giving birth to children. The adding of this intense pain to childbearing could have been indicative to the pain that was inflicted upon humanity through this act of sin.

She would also be made to be subject to her husband. The Bible clearly states, "...he will rule over you" (Gen. 3:16). From this time forward, God established an order of humanity that would make women subject to the authority men (1 Cor. 11:3-9).

Adam was sentenced to a life of hard work. The ground would not be cultivated easily. It would need constant attention from Adam in order for it to yield its harvest. In addition, he is sentenced to physical death. The decay of the body was set in motion.

This began the initial judgement of sin upon Satan and humanity. The effects of this sentence would be felt by every individual who would ever live (Rom. 5:12). It would take the efforts of a loving God and Savior to deliver humankind from this dreadful verdict.

Sin would further be judged by the Savior upon the cross (John 1:29; 2 Cor. 5:21; 1 Pet. 2:24). As Jesus was hanging upon the cross, God considered him to be sin for us. His death was for the purpose of God inflicting judgement upon sin. There is no logical way for any believer to say, "I could not help myself" because Christ gave sin a deathblow upon the cross (Rom. 6:11, 12).

The Bible speaks of him being beaten for our deliverance. It states, "...*by His scourging we are healed*" (Isa. 53:5). This should be interpreted as spiritual healing not physical. The marks and cuts left on Christ's body when he was beaten resulted in the opportunity for any person who believed in Christ to be spiritually healed from the wounds sin left upon us.

Furthermore, sin is being judged daily. No one is exempt from succumbing to the effects of sin. Although we are born again, we still have to deal with the acts of sin and will continue to deal with overcoming the propensity to sin until we are redeemed from these physical bodies (Matt. 16:24; Gal. 5:24).

According to First Corinthians, a believer should examine his life daily to deal with sin (1 Cor. 11:31). If we consistently do this, we will escape future penalty (Heb. 12:6-11). If not, there is certain punishment that awaits every believer.

The judgement of sin remains a future aspect for all people who refuse to repose their faith in Jesus Christ. There is a day coming when God will conclude His act of judging sin in the lives of people. It will begin with the pouring out of His wrath and will be concluded with judgement at the great white throne (1 Thes. 1:10; Rev. 20:11-15).

Presently, God's complete judgement against sin is being restrained so that He can save as many as will repent (Rom. 2:4-6; 2 Pet. 3:9). However, those who refuse to repent, thereby accepting Christ's judgement of sin, can expect to experience the day of God's wrath (Rev. 6:12-17).

The Judgement Seat of Christ

The first judgement of people in the next age will begin with the "household of God" at the judgement seat of Christ (1 Pet. 4:17). At the bema, there will be retribution for every good and wicked deed done by saints.

The word "judgement" is pronounced *bema* in the Greek. It is a seat situated on a raised platform. There are two predominant views of Christ's judgement seat.

First, it is viewed as the scene of a courtroom. If you have ever been in one, you should have noticed that the seat of the judge is raised from all other seats in the room. The judge is the person who will give the final ruling on any case that comes before them.

The proponents of this view believe that both good and bad deeds will be addressed. The judgement will either be to one's advantage or disadvantage.

The second perspective is that of an athlete who has won a competition. They are to come before the seat of the judge, be inspected and receive their rewards (1 Cor. 9:24-27; 2 Tim. 2:5). Those who hold to this paradigm believe that only rewards or loss of them will be addressed. For the most part, they do not believe that there will be any retribution for the believer who lived an ungodly life.

There are three major texts that refer to the judgement seat of Christ. In these passages, Paul states that we (believers only) will appear before Christ's judgement seat to give an account of the things we did in our body.

In Romans, the apostle makes the statement, *"...we will all stand before the judgement seat of God/Christ"* (Rom. 14:10). The context of the passage is dealing with some believers who judge others in regards to what they eat. Paul relates that our focus should not be on what a brother is eating. More importantly, we should be concerned about giving an account to Christ about what we have done with our lives.

You must be aware that your life is one of preparation. You ultimately determine how judgement will go for yourself based upon how you lived your life.

This reality should cause us to live in a way that will allow Christ to declare that we have been "good", "good and faithful" or "faithful and wise" servants (Matt. 25:14-30; Luke 12:42, 19:17).

In another passage, Paul states that there will be believers at the bema who have done "good or bad" (2 Cor. 5:9, 10). This verse undoubtedly says that there are believers who stand before Christ that have lived lives pleasing to God while others have been displeasing.

What is interesting to note is that Christ pays his servants what they earned. We earn both our reward and punishment. Worldliness is the greatest issue that warrants punishment at the judgement seat.

Paul writes these two verses within the context of talking about the physical body. This present body is temporal, and decaying like an old garment. Physical deterioration was not a tragedy for him; it was a point of excitement and anticipation.

The apostle knew that when he left his earthly body, he would appear before the Lord with a different one. Therefore he lived this present life with the expectation of being pleasing to God. If Paul knew that he was pleasing to God on Earth, he would subsequently be pleasing to Him at the judgement seat (2 Tim. 4:6-8).

The word "receive" in Second Corinthians 5:10 means that a person is receiving back what belongs to him. After examination at the judgement seat, the Lord will give back to you what is rightfully yours. You could receive either rewards or punishment based upon your good or bad deeds.

Good deeds are the things you do which are upright and honorable; therefore, pleasing to God. Again, your works consist of thoughts, words and actions. How you think about a person is examined just as much as what you do for them.

In contrast, bad deeds are things that are evil, wicked, depraved or harmful. This would be anything that contradicts God or impedes your progress of spiritual growth (Heb. 12:1).

Paul concludes this segment with the phrase, *"Knowing the fear of the Lord, we persuade men"* (2 Cor. 5:11).This is the bottom line. The Lord is to be feared (Luke 12:4, 5). The day of trial at the judgement seat is one that should not be taken lightly (Luke 19:20-27).

This was the reason why Paul worked so diligently to "persuade men" to live righteously. There is great retribution to come on believers who lived ungodly lives. Therefore, he used every ounce of grace in his life to win men to Christ, escaping the "terror of the Lord".

God is not letting people get away with anything. We tell our children if they do something wrong it's going to get ugly for them. This is exactly what will happen if your life is not right. It's going to be ugly for you at the bema.

As preachers, we want to motivate people to achieve great things; however, we must not preach a watered down and polluted gospel. It is incumbent upon us to share in such a way as to bring people into accountability with Christ. Our goal should be to avert as many believers away from the "terror of the Lord" as we can.

The final passage to be considered gives us a perspective of how Christ will categorize our works. Everything in our lives will be divided into two groups. There is "gold, silver, precious stones" or "wood, hay, stubble." Depending upon what group our works are in, we will either gain or lose a rewards (1 Cor. 3:11-15).

Gold, silver and precious stones refer to the purity of what you believe and do. What determines the value of gold and silver is how much your works have been purified. The more you submit your life to Christ, the less your flesh (sinful nature) gets involved in what you do. Everything you do should be you are submitted and obedient to the leading of the Holy Spirit. This will ensure that your works are of the purest quality.

These metals and stones refer to something that is worth a great price. The only thing that we have which can truly be counted of great price is our life. This is what Christ examines. Purified works are those that emanate from the Divine life within you.

In contrast, wood, hay and stubble represent the things about our lives that are worthless. This refers to what you believe and do. Those things which fail to build up others' faith and minister grace are reputed worthless by Christ resulting in loss of reward (2 Jn. 1:8; Rev. 3:11).

The issue of judgement of believers is for you a reward or punishment because of how productive you were for the kingdom of God.

This examination will be a fiery ordeal. The believer who lived a life which contributed to their great loss will still be saved "yet so as through fire" (1 Cor. 3:15). Through this trial by fire, you may lose your reward, but still are guaranteed salvation because of your foundation – Christ. This fiery ordeal will be horrific.

Christ intends to put pain on disobedient believers. However, because of his great love for the saints, he will make sure that none experience the lake of fire. God's grace is powerful enough to keep us but that is not good enough. If you are not productive as a believer, certain punishment awaits you at the judgement seat of Christ.

Three Ranks of Overcomers

After Christ judges the saints that his bema, he will assign three levels of ranks to those who will rule with him in the millennial kingdom.

The first level is classified as the "good servant" (Luke 19:17). The issue Jesus discusses in passage has to do his citizens opinion of him. They did not want Jesus to reign over them. Such is the case for many in the church today.

Many recognize him as Savior but not Lord. Only complete submission to his Lordship guarantees access into the future visible kingdom. Although they did not submit to the King, they were still his citizens. This means they were believers.

The Lordship of Christ is expressed through your submission to leadership. Some people are easily offended when their pastor addresses issues in their lives. They walk around as if to say, "Who do you think you are?" and "I am grown." This attitude reflects their lack of submission to the Lordship of Jesus Christ.

I have watched people leave the church because their pastor told them they were not ready for a certain aspect of ministry. They say God told them to attend their particular church, but when they do not want to hear what the pastor has to say they don't wait for God to tell them to leave the church. This is typical non-compliance to the Lordship of Jesus Christ.

After the King returned, ready to rule in his kingdom, he called his servants to investigate what they had done with what he had given them (Luke 19:15). The issue that Christ will be concerned with is - are you productive. Lazy Christians will not inherit the kingdom of God. However, root reason why believers are not productive is because they do not acknowledge his Lordship.

The reward for being a "good slave" is to rule over cities. The King gave 10 cities to one servant and five to another (Luke 19:17-18). The cities represent territories that Christ delegates to the good slaves.

When the Lord returns, he will give territory in the kingdom to those who have been faithful for the kingdom now. Believers who are impervious to the reality that Christ is coming to establish his kingdom will not rule with him when he returns (Rev. 2:26-27).

Notice, Christ gave all the servants the same amount of money – 10 pounds. However, one servant was more productive than the others. He gives everyone the same amount of money because it represents the completed work of Christ.

After salvation, some believers work harder than others to advance the kingdom of God; therefore, Christ gives them a greater reward.

The next class of overcomers is referred to as the "good and faithful" servant (Matt. 25:14). In this parable, Christ presents the issue of faithfulness. He has assigned each one of us duties based upon the talents he has invested in our lives. We must find out what he is requiring of us and fulfill that mission. That determines if we are actually faithful to him.

Although this story is similar to the parable of the pounds, you must look very closely to distinguish the subtle differences. In the parable of the pounds, the King gave all of the servants the same amount of money, whereas in this parable of the talents, the King gave different amounts to each slave (Matt. 25:15).

In this parable the King considered each person's individual ability and then gave them money. The amounts differ here because the issue is not the completed work of Christ. It is the special abilities that God is giving you as a servant.

It is up to you to use your abilities to advance the kingdom of God. It does not matter how many talents you have. You must be productive with whatever God has invested in your life. Both the servant with 10 talents and the one with five talents doubled what they had. Therefore, Christ gave them the same reward.

The "good servants" received cities as their reward. Here, Christ made the "good and faithful" servant ruler over many things. This seems to be more than just cities. Do you see the progression? The first group of servants obtains cities while the next receives many things.

The final rank of overcomers consists of the "faithful and wise" (Matt. 24:45). In addition to being faithful, these believers are also wise. There is a major difference between this group of servants and the other two.

The "good" and the "good and faithful" servants were in possession of what they had personally. However, Christ considers these servants to be "faithful and wise" because they have to deal with other people. The responsibility of these individuals is to govern the household of God.

It requires a sufficient amount of wisdom to cause God's people to become kingdom seekers. These servants are given the highest reward of all – everything (Matt. 24:47). The "faithful and wise" servants will have the privilege of governing all of Christ's substance.

If you have enough wisdom to govern souls, which have eternal value, then Christ will let you rule over everything he has. This is the greatest reward you can obtain. So, there are the "good" servants who rule over cities, the "good and faithful" servants who rule over much and the "faithful and wise" servants who rule over everything. Each parable illustrates how Christ will classify overcoming believers at his judgement seat. The bottom line Christ will be considering is how productive were you in your perspective assignment.

Jesus Christ was not attempting to find out were they saved. He already knew that. This is why he called them servants. What Jesus Christ will demand of you at the bema are the facts of how productive you were in this life. The greatest indictment against the people of God is to be trifling or lazy. To be saved 5, 10 or 20 years with little fruit to show for it will result in great punishment.

Rewards

Crowns

One prominent reward in the Bible is the bestowing of crowns. There are five noted in the Scriptures. These are incorruptible, rejoicing, righteousness, life and exultation. These crowns represent your personal victory in life over your flesh, how much of an impact you had on other peoples' lives and that you completed the responsibility handed to you by Christ. Crowns will become a mark of distinction by which Christ has honored those who have been faithful to him in this life.

It is debated as to whether these are literal crowns or stars within the crown. In whatever way you view them, it is certain that they represent honor given to every believer who has devoted their life to serving Christ in every way possible.

Paul speaks of the incorruptible crown within the analogy of running a race. In the public games, the victors were awarded a crown or wreath. Paul uses this image to relate to us that everyone who disciplines his life will receive the prize of an incorruptible crown (1 Cor. 9:24-27).

He further uses the analogy of a boxer. Just like the skilled boxer carefully places his punches so that he does not miss his opponent, so the apostle lived his life directing it towards the specific goal of gaining the prize.

To do so he had to exercise self-control in all things. In other words, he had to live by the rules that govern the Christian life. Only then could he be certain that he would become the victor (2 Tim. 2:5).

You and I can win this crown by imposing sanctions on

what we do. Paul made this statement, *"I discipline my body and make it my slave..."* (1 Cor. 9:27). This means that he disciplined his body through hardships.

Because Paul did not want Christ to reject him at the judgement seat, there were certain things that he simply would not allow himself to do. There are guidelines that govern the Christian life. If you want to receive this crown, you must make sure you live your life according to these regulations as recorded in the Word of God.

Christ gives the crown of rejoicing to the overseer of any assembly who faithfully ministers to the Chief Shepherd's sheep and becomes an example of how they should live (1 Pet. 5:1-4). Only elders and above can receive this crown.

It is always a good aspiration to become a leader within the assembly. However, money, power nor prestige can be your ambition for entering the ministry. To attempt to control and manipulate God's people for your gain is unacceptable (1 Cor. 11:1; Philip. 3:17).

As a leader, you should exemplify impeccable faithfulness to Christ in all aspects of your life by which those under your leadership can follow.

There is another crown referred to as the crown of righteousness. In Second Timothy, Paul states that he has accomplished three things: (A) he has fought a good fight, (B) he has finished his course and (C) he has kept the faith. This shows us how to obtain the crown of righteousness (2 Tim. 4:7, 8).

You must be a person who overcomes any struggle, dangers or obstacles that impede the progress of holiness and the spreading of the gospel. You must stay focused on your course of life endeavoring with every ounce of energy to complete it.

In addition, you must hold firmly to the faith (Jude 1:6). Things and people can become a distraction to you. The only way to maintain your grasp on the faith is captured in the phrase "love His appearing" (2 Tim. 4:8). Your love for Christ and your reflection on him as the righteous judge will help you stay focused.

Next is the crown of life (James 1:12). Christ gives this reward to the person who does not succumb to the untimely desires of the flesh – temptations. When thoughts enter into your mind to do things that you know contradicts what it means to be a Christian, you must reject them. This is what it means to overcome temptation.

The word "perseveres" in the epistle of James chapter one verse twelve gives the emphasis of dealing with temptation bravely and calmly. You can neither be afraid nor act irrationally about the temptations that confront you.

You must become like the colonel who remains calm while bullets are flying over his head in war, to achieve the goal set before him. Overcoming temptation is spiritual warfare. To be victorious, you must look ahead to the goal – Christ.

Temptation is the enticement to sin. Let's be clear about something. There is pleasure in sin (Heb. 11:25). You are primarily tempted by the things that are enjoyable to you.

This is the danger of temptation. It is also the reason why you must deal with it bravely and calmly. Overcoming temptation is a difficult task. The only way you will continuously overcome it is because you "love him" (James 1:12).

Finally, there is the crown of exultation (1 Thes. 2:19). Paul asks the question, *"For who is our hope or joy or crown of exultation?"* He concludes that the people whom he has converted to the Lord were the source of his hope, joy and rejoicing. Christ will acknowledge everyone's effort to lead unbelievers to him.

The apostle spent his life preaching Christ to the Gentiles. Although he experienced many hardships and trials, he would not be deterred from pursuing those who needed the Savior. Through constantly visiting and revisiting those whom he made disciples of Christ, he strengthened them in order that they would not be shaken from faith in Christ Jesus (Acts 14:22).

As Paul taught them, their spiritual strength grew. The converts' lives began to imitate Christ all the more. They would not be distracted from their pursuit of the kingdom of God and his glory (1 Thes. 2:11-13). Consequently, the stability of these disciples would become the source of Paul's joy and rejoicing in the presence of the Lord during his second coming because they represented his work for Christ.

As we pursue individuals, converting them to Christ, strengthening their faith in him, we can have confidence concerning the day of Christ's return. Those we win to him will become proof to Christ that our lives were about helping him in the process of recovering humankind. The disciples of Christ will become our "crown of exultation".

These crowns are given to every servant of Christ who exceeds the efforts of the status quo of believers.

Access into the Millennial Kingdom

Christ grants us permission to enter his millennial kingdom. Living a righteous life does not guarantee us salvation. This is the secured possession of every believer because of the completed work of Christ (Gal. 2:16; Eph. 2:8, 9; Philip. 3:9). However, we do strive to live a holy life, laying aside every weight and sin with the goal of gaining entrance into the Christ's millennial kingdom (Gal. 5:19-21; 2 Pet. 1:10, 11). This is not eternity. It is the reward of participating in the future millennial reign of Christ is the next age.

Reigning Over Cities

Earlier, we discussed this aspect of reward briefly. I want to discuss it in a little further detail. The overcoming believers will rule over cities/nations. This reward is greatly overlooked. The Scripture give us an indication that some overcoming believers will be given positions of great authority in the kingdom of Christ (Ps. 8:6; Luke 19:12-26; Rev. 2:27).

Some will rule over ten cities. Others will rule over five cities. Each overcoming servant of Christ will become a governor over territory and people because they have been found faithful in executing Christ's affairs here on Earth.

The book of Revelation further shows that their authority will allow them to bring harsh judgement upon the nations that refuse to worship Christ. They will rule every nation under their authority with a "rod of iron".

The Greek rendering of the word "rod" speaks of a shepherd's rod. These overcomers shall rule the nations like a shepherd who is guarding his sheep. The triumphant saints will know how to have a firm but gentle rule (Ps. 2:9).

The Wedding Feast

All prevailing saints will have unhindered fellowship with Christ at the wedding feast (Matt. 22:1-14; Rev. 19:7-9). Both of the above passages are a description of the same event. Matthew gives us a description of the entire process. Revelation gives us a description of what qualifies one to be given access to this fellowship.

In the gospel of Matthew, Jesus tells the story of a king who was putting together a marriage feast for his son. The king obviously is God whereas the son is Christ Jesus. This wedding feast is a future event that occurs immediately preceding the initiation of the millennial kingdom of Christ. As you study the text, you can see that there were different groups of people involved in this gathering.

The king sent two groups of messengers out to invite people to the wedding but many of them walked away, refusing, while the remaining remnant slaughtered the king's servants (Matt. 22:1-6). Those violent men portrayed in this parable were none other than the Jews who refused the invitation of Jesus Christ and continually fought against the call of the prophets and apostles to share in his kingdom. After the Jews refused the king's request, everyone else was invited.

The Gentiles are now brought into perspective (Matt. 22:9, 10). Here we see the work of the New Testament ministry. God intends to accept any person who desires to fellowship with his son. At the preaching of the king's servants, the wedding was furnished with guests, but there was a problem.

As the king entered the room, he saw one of the guests not properly dressed for the feast. When questioned about his attire, the person was speechless. The visitor was then removed from the feast and cast into outer darkness (Matt. 22:11-13).

When the book of Revelation speaks of this wedding, it states that the *"bride has made herself ready"* (Rev. 19:7). In one sense we are prepared through Christ's righteousness; in the other, we prepare ourselves through our own righteousness (1 Cor. 1:30; Philip. 3:9; Rev. 19:8). The garment worn at the wedding is based upon your personal righteousness.

The phrase "righteousness of saints" in some translations should be more correctly understood as the "righteous acts of the saints" (Rev. 19:8). "Righteousness" is defined as a person's deeds or actions. In the Greek, the word is written in plural form and should be read as "righteousnesses."

You prepare your garment through living a righteous life and bearing spiritual fruit. Accordingly, if there is no righteousness in your life, there will be no garment you to wear.

Praise and Honor

When the judgement of believers is complete, every devotee of Christ whose faith endured fiery trials receives special praise, honor and glory (1 Pet. 1:7).

Praise is God's commendation of approval (Rom. 2:29). Honor will be apparent in the bestowing of future rewards. Glory will be reflective of Christ's opinion of us (2 Pet. 1:17). All three of these aspects will become the reward of the believer in the future kingdom.

A Glorified Body

As a reward, every believer's body will have varying degrees of glory (Rom. 8:30; 2 Cor. 4:17, 18; Col. 3:4). This is the physical expression of God's glory. However, some saints will have a greater expression of His glory than others because of their faithfulness in enduring trials and converting others to righteousness (Dan. 12:3; Rom. 8:17, 18).

The book of Romans says that this appearance of glory is given to the special believers who become "fellow-heirs" with Christ. This means that Christ allows you to experience the same glory he has because of your willingness to identify with him in the aspect of suffering. Daniel chapter twelve verse three adds further light on this subject. He wrote that the "wise" believers who died in the faith will rise, becoming luminaries of Christ. Some believers who were diligent about the work of Christ will shine "as the stars".

Punishment

Rejection from the Kingdom

Christ will exclude some members of his body from his millennial kingdom. Participation in the future kingdom is a privilege, not necessarily your right. A saint is given access into the kingdom not because they have faith in Christ but because they are **worthy** (Matt. 22:8; 2 Thes. 1:5; Rev. 3:4).

The word "worthy" literally means deserving. The kingdom is only given to those who have proven themselves deserving of it. This does not mean that one believer is better than the other is. It merely points out that one person has loved God so much until they have disciplined themselves in preparation to experience the complete work of salvation. Spiritual recovery is not just about making it into eternity. It is about enjoying blessed fellowship with the Savior in every aspect.

Being Disinherited

As another aspect of discipline, God will disinherit unfaithful believers. When I write of being disinherited, I am talking about the blessings and rewards in addition to salvation. There are several passages of scripture that give the impression that at least some part of what God has reserved as an inheritance for believers can be taken away.

In Matthew's gospel, the Lord had returned to judge his servants (Matt. 25:24-28). After judging the first two, he expressed his pleasure. However, upon examining the third, the Lord expressed extreme displeasure. The Lord's final recommendation concerning that worker was *"Take away the talent from him, and give it to the one who has the ten talents...from the one who does not have, even what he does have shall be taken away."*

In the millennium, we will be delegated certain responsibilities as a reward based upon how much Christ was able to trust us in serving him now. Because the third servant did not help in advancing the kingdom of God at all, he lost his ability to serve Christ in the future.

The worker who proved himself to be faithful in Christ's work before judgement occurred gained the portion of reward which the wicked and lazy servant lost (Luke 19:20-26).

The loss of rewards is a reality, which is why the apostle John admonished his readers to make sure that they receive a full reward. *"Watch yourselves, that you do not lose what we have accomplished, but that you may receive a **full** reward"* (2 Jn. 1:8). John cautions his readers to consider their life. He could have instructed them to make sure they did the proper things to remain "saved" but he did not. He was concerned with them gaining a complete reward.

John knew that the saints were working hard to receive a reward from Christ. Yet, he writes that what they were working for could be "lost". What could be lost – the reward. Every believer who is dedicating their life in service to Christ must make sure that they do not lose what they have worked so very hard to receive – a full reward.

The book of Revelation gives us a statement that additionally reflects that a Christian can be disinherited (Rev. 3:11). It states, *"I am coming quickly; **hold fast** what you have so that no one will take your crown."* Obviously, this pertains to the future judgement of the saints. The Lord himself encourages us to keep possession of what we have worked to receive – a crown.

You must hold on to your reward securely. The process of living a victorious Christian life is a long one. It is easy to begin working for God with great zeal without enduring to the end, understanding that making it to the finish matters just as much as our beginning. If you fail to stay focused on the reward, you will ultimately fall to the wayside.

A Word about Hell

Before discussing the last two elements of punishment for believers, I want to discuss the subject of Hell. The next two sections dealing with punishment define where Christ will send some believers. The King James Version of the Bible refers to one of the places as Hell. The difficult thing is to understand what Hell is since the English language has translated three different Greek words as the same English word Hell. Therefore, without having some knowledge of the Greek language you will miss key revelation about the destination of some believers. The English word Hell translates in the Greek as Gehenna, Hades or Tartarus.

I do believe that some believers will go to Hell. However, it is not Hades it is Gehenna. It is not an eternal punishment. It is a temporal punishment which lasts for 1000 years. Any discipline Christ hands out to believers will not last for eternity. This dispensational discipline will begin and end at the start and conclusion of the millennial kingdom.

Hades is merely a holding place for the departed souls of unbelievers. This is not punishment for them, it is simply a place of holding until they experience judgement. At the conclusion of the judgements, everyone in Hell (Hades) is released to undergo judgement at the great white throne (Rev. 20:13). Their judgement will culminate with the eternal destination of the lake of fire.

Pay very close attention here. Everyone unredeemed person who dies immediately finds himself or herself in Hell (Hades). However, no saint goes to Hell (Gehenna) until after he or she appears at the judgement seat of Christ. In one scenario, people are occupying Hell presently when they die. In the other, no one will occupy it until after Christ's judgement seat. Hades is not judgement for unbelievers. However, Gehenna is judgement for saints.

Gary Whipple defines Gehenna as, "A region of destruction and ruin, which will contain fire, the graves of the slain bodies of apostates, and the blackness of darkness where bodiless souls will be confined. At the end of the thousand years its inhabitants will be raised and changed, along with those who had been confined alive in the region of the outer darkness."

Gehenna refers to the valley of Hinnom in the Old

Testament. It is a temporal place of punishment for apostate believers. In the Bible, it was the place of judgement for criminals located near Jerusalem. All types of filth and rubbish was thrown into Gehenna and burned.

God slaughtered His own people because of their apostasy and placed their dead bodies in the valley of Hinnom (Gehenna). It was in the Valley of Hinnom that Ahaz burnt incense in worship to other gods and burnt some of the children in the fire as a sacrifice (2 Chr. 28:1-4; Jer. 19:1-6).

God renamed this place the Valley of slaughter. He did not kill His people there. They were slain elsewhere and He placed the bodies of the slaughtered individuals there as part of their judgement (Jer. 7:30-32). Gehenna then, in essence, is a graveyard where Christ will place all the bodies of slain apostate believers after he has judged them at his judgement seat.

If you are a believer who attends church regularly or even sometimes and you continue to live in sin such as living with someone you are not married to, this is not where Christ will send you. You will be sent to outer darkness. Gehenna is only for people who believed in Jesus and departed from the faith to worship another god. The Bible refers to these people as apostate believers. They will experience the severest discipline at the judgement seat of Christ – the second death for believers.

The second death for believers means that some will experience two deaths. The first death is that of the physical body. The second death will occur at the judgement seat of Christ (Rev. 2:11). This is the slaying of the believer and placing the body in Gehenna while sending the soul to the blackness of darkness. See the section on the second death.

If someone says to you as a believer, "If you continue living the way you are you are going to Hell", ask them which Hell are they referring to. As a believer, if you apostatize, you will go to Gehenna not Hades.

The introduction of this concept occurred when Jesus was preaching his sermon on the mountain. This was the first time Jesus discussed the rules that govern the kingdom. Everything you read in Matthew chapters 5 through 7 refers to inclusion or exclusion from the millennial kingdom.

Jesus says that one of the judgements for believers who violate the rules that govern the kingdom is Hell. Although the word Hell appears in the King James Version of the Bible, the Greek word is Gehenna (Matt. 5:22). Remember, Jesus addressed this message to believers. Therefore, this is not a final judgement upon them. Again, no punishment for believers is eternal.

Matthew chapter ten verse twenty-eight states, *"Do not fear those who kill the body but are unable to kill the soul; but rather fear Him who is able to destroy both soul and body in Hell."* Notice, for apostate believers, Christ sends both their body and soul to Hell. The Greek word there is also Gehenna.

Christ was warning believers about departing from the faith because of the immense and intense trials they would experience. If they became disciples of another after following him, they would experience the most severe judgement – Gehenna. Christ only places the body in Gehenna. The soul of apostate believers goes to the black darkness. See discussion on the black darkness.

If believers understand what judgement Christ will

impose on them because of their apostasy, they would reconsider their decision. This reality should be enough to make sure you stay in the Way. Whatever, your struggles, hardships or mistreatment, do not depart from the faith in search of another religion (1 Tim. 4:1).

Outer Darkness

Christ will command the angels to cast unproductive believers into outer darkness. This phrase occurs only three times in the Bible. Every mention of "outer darkness" is recorded in the Gospel of Matthew and pertains to the dispensational punishment of believers (Matt. 8:12, 22:13, 25:30). By looking at these scriptures, you can tell that this judgement will occur prior to the beginning of the marriage supper (Rev. 19:7-10). Christ will send all believers whom he excludes from the wedding feast to either Gehenna or outer darkness.

What exactly is outer darkness? It is a dispensational chastisement for believers. Outer darkness is a region located somewhere outside the kingdom. The people there will be able to see the lighted palace of Christ; however, they are excluded from enjoying fellowship with him in it.

All non-overcoming believers will spend 1000 years in the outer darkness while all overcoming believers enjoy the millennial kingdom.

Placing these believers just outside the light of the kingdom causes great grief to them because they will have a view of the kingdom but be eliminated from participation in it. They are allowed to be spectators but not participators. This is a huge reason why there will be "weeping and gnashing of teeth".

The phrase "weeping and gnashing of teeth" gives more

indication of their agony (Luke 13:28). They will be crying in conjunction with grinding their teeth. This is extreme anguish and despair. The rejected believers see the light of the kingdom but are forbidden to enjoy it. At that time, it will be apparent what living a disciplined and productive life would have secured them.

Outer darkness is different from the blackness of darkness. Outer darkness is the place of judgement for all believers who were not overcomers; yet, they never left the Christian faith. The blackness of darkness is strictly for all believers who commit apostasy. Although they are different judgements, each one is dispensational or temporary.

Outer darkness is not Hell or the lake of fire either. It cannot be either of these. Hell (Hades) is the holding place of all unbelievers until they are consigned to eternal damnation in the lake of fire (Luke 16:22, 23; Rev. 20:12-14). Outer darkness is a temporal place of punishment for believers.

Both places are for temporary use. The first is being used now to accommodate everyone who died as an unbeliever. However, there will be no need for Hell after the great white throne judgement (Rev. 20:14). Outer darkness will be used later as a place of judgement for all believers excluded from the kingdom.

It cannot be the lake of fire either. The mention of fire precludes that there will be some degree of light. Consequently, it cannot be "outer darkness". The lake of fire is the final destination of all unbelievers.

As it pertains to the eternal punishment of the wicked and the temporal punishment of the just, they are both **cast** into their respective place of judgement. However, Christ will cast believers into outer darkness **before** the millennium, whereas he will cast the wicked into the lake of fire **after** the millennium.

Each reference in Matthew to "outer darkness" shows us why these believers were consigned to this judgement. The first instance is found recorded in Matthew chapter eight verse twelve. This reference pertains strictly to the Jews who are called "children of the kingdom".

The promise of the kingdom was originally given to them. However, they did not possess the faith to trust that God was establishing it through Jesus Christ. Consequently, all unbelieving Jews will be cast into outer darkness.

The next passage is found in Matthew chapter twenty-two verses one through fourteen. Here is a picture of the future wedding feast. The second reason why a person finds themselves in outer darkness is because they did not live a righteous life (Matt. 5:20). Yes, we are eternally secured, but this fact though does not give us liberty to live ungodly lives. There are stiff penalties every believer will experience due to ungodliness and sin remaining in their life. One of them is outer darkness.

The guest at the wedding feast was first bound and then thrown into outer darkness (Matt. 22:13). To "bind hand and foot" means to place chains upon this servant. Not only will he or she be in outer darkness; even their mobility is taken from them. Not even the worst of unbelievers kept in Hell until their judgement are put in chains.

It is a great offence to Christ for him to die in order that we might be rescued from death to enjoy eternal fellowship with him and then refuse to live a life worthy of this great blessing. This servant is dealt with the most severely because the most grievous offence is a lack of personal righteousness.

The third reason why a believer is cast into outer darkness is that they are "wicked and lazy" (Matt. 25:24-30). They are wicked because of their attitude towards the work of the kingdom. This wrong attitude is also the cause of their laziness. Basically, the Lord finds that the believers of this category are "unprofitable" to him.

The Lord intends to delegate authority to responsible and productive disciples (Matt. 25:20-23; Luke 19:12-19). If you are not profitable to him now, how can He trust you to be profitable to Him then? The emphasis of these parables is not on how gifted you are rather, how productive you were in the kingdom.

There will also be degrees of punishment handed out in outer darkness. In Matthew chapter twenty-two verse thirteen, the Lord commands his servants (the angels) to take the man who was not dressed for the wedding and "bind him hand and foot", whereas the servant in Matthew chapter twenty-five verse thirty was merely cast into outer darkness. The last servant was not bound whatsoever. The parable of the Wedding Feast is the only instance in the gospels where Christ commands one of his servants to be bound and thrown into outer darkness.

Beaten

Christ will beat all non-overcoming believers. There is a story in Luke about being a "faithful" and "wise" servant (Luke 12:41-48). While there are some servants of Christ who have committed themselves to serving others the Word in the kingdom of God, some leaders do just the opposite. They not only mistreated and abused the people of God; they also become indulgent in the fleshly aspects of life concluding that their master will not return quickly.

Luke chapter twelve verse forty-six says that these insensible servants will be "cut in pieces". This does not mean put to death by cutting into pieces. It means that this servants beating for this rebellion and apostasy will be so severe that it will literally tear their flesh in pieces.

Beating was a common practice in the Old Testament for disciplining any person considered to be wicked (Deut. 25:2, 3). The person could receive up to 40 lashes for their offense. This kept the punishment from becoming inhumane.

There will be those who are beaten with "many stripes" or "few strips". Those who did not know the Lord's will concerning serving his people with the Word but still violated it will also be beaten. However, theirs will not be as brutal.

It is difficult to understand that the Lord will beat even those servants who did not know his will but yet violated it. Yet, this reflects the fact that there will be varying degrees of punishment and that Christ will not accept any excuse of "I didn't know". The Lord will not tolerate any ignorance. You must not abuse the knowledge you have. You must also continue working to experience as much revelation of the will of God as you can.

The important aspect of this passage is that you must give to others what you receive from God to help them advance. You can be neither selfish nor scared to help improve the quality of spiritual life for others.

Second Death for Believers

This second death is similar to the first (physical death); it is the separation of the soul and the body at the judgement seat of Christ. The body is sent to Gehenna whereas the soul is sent to the black darkness (Jude 1:13). The second death will be applicable to the believers and unbelievers alike.

Although the second death affects two different groups of people, the consequences they yield are completely different. The second death for unbelievers is eternal. The second death for believers is temporal. The second death for believers is what we will discuss. The book of Revelation states, *"...he who overcomes will not be hurt by the second death"* (Rev. 2:11).

The Bible is not referring to unbelievers because this message is to the church of Smyrna. Jesus uses the word "overcome" to differentiate between those who will endure their trials instead of abandoning their faith. The believers who succumb to the pressures of their great trials, looking elsewhere to gain release from their suffering, will suffer a second death.

It is difficult to fathom that God will raise believers from the dead to stand before Christ only for some of them to die again because of their apostasy. This is the case none-the-less.

The other reference to the second death is located in Revelation chapter twenty verse six. *"Blessed and holy is the one who has a part in the first resurrection; over these the second death has no power, but they will be priests of God and of Christ and will reign with Him for a thousand years."*

According to this scripture, if you are exempt from reigning with Christ, you can experience the second death. Everyone Christ deems worthy to reign escapes the second death. This second death is a second dying according to the gospel of Luke (Luke 19:27). For believers, the second death does not culminate in the lake of fire.

At the judgement seat, Christ will give the command to kill some believers. Again, this is the second death for believers. Jesus himself makes this statement, *"But these enemies of mine, who did not want me to reign over them, bring them here and slay them in my presence"* (Luke 19:27).

As you read the narrative of the servants whom Jesus Christ entrusted money to, you will find a select group of his citizens refused to have him reign over them. They rejected his rule because of their sheer hate for him (Luke 19:14).

These are not unbelievers. First, even though they hated him, Jesus considered them his citizens, which means he had every right to rule over them.

Secondly, the King judged these citizens in the exact same spot where he rewarded the faithful servants. This is what he means by "bring them here". If this was the judgement seat of Christ for the faithful servants; surely, it became the judgement seat of Christ for the citizens who hated their King.

Christ's citizens became his enemies because they rejected his rule. That is, they departed from the faith. This level of punishment coincides with the greatest reward Christ gives to the "faithful and wise" servants.

He allows the faithful ones to rule over all his possessions while he kills the evil citizens. Christ does not kill all defeated believers at the judgement seat. However, this select group however, Christ determines that they should die.

The word "slay" in Luke chapter 19 actually means to kill. This is the second death. If you fall into this category, Christ will raise you from the dead to stand amongst believers at judgement. However, you will die again and your body will be sent to Gehenna.

The Blackness of Darkness

When God places the body in Gehenna, He will send the soul to a place called the "black darkness" or the "blackness of darkness". Some theologians believe this is also located in the region of Gehenna.

There are two passages where the blackness of darkness is mentioned. You can find the first comment about the blackness of darkness in Second Peter chapter two verse seventeen. The apostle Peter writes, *"These are springs without water and mists driven by a storm, for whom the black darkness has been reserved."*

The other mention of the blackness of darkness is located in the epistle of Jude. He writes, *"Wild waves of the sea, casting up their own shame like foam; wandering stars, for whom the black darkness has been reserved for ever."* Both of these passages refer to apostate believers.

The black darkness literally means the densest darkness. The place where God is going to put these apostate believers is the worst darkness that exists. This corresponds to Tartarus for the rebellious angels. God confined them in the deepest darkest part of Hades. This is the most severe judgement that will be given to any believer and displays Christ's great anger for any believer who departs from the faith and teaches others to do the same. This is not Hell. We discovered that Hell is only a holding place for the unrighteous. This is not the lake of fire. The fact that there is fire present means that there cannot be darkness there. Therefore, the blackness of darkness must be some other place God assigns believers to as punishment. I believe this is where God sends soul of the apostate believer while confining the body in Gehenna.

As you examine the Scripture closely, it is evident that these people are apostate believers. Peter says that these people are teachers of heresy. It is their intention to deceive people from loyalty to Christ. They also deny their master Christ (2 Pet. 2:1). This literally means they have apostacized from God and Christ. In fact, Peter says that they follow Balaam. The Jews considered this as the worst way to abandon Christ.

Jude adds to this description (Jude 1:12-13). They are "hidden reefs in you love feast..." They cause moral wreck to believers. They are "clouds without water". They promise refreshing truth but have none to give. They are "autumn trees whose fruit" meaning they are unfruitful and worthless. They are "wild waves of the sea". They are impulsive man motivated by ungodly desires. Finally, they are "wandering stars". This gives the greatest indication as to what they have done. By wandering stars, Jude means that they have departed from the course God has laid out for them and have decided to live life based upon what they want to do. All of these characteristics define one person who has become an apostate believer. For them, God has prepared the place of the black darkness.

The Judgement of the Nations

You must distinguish the difference between the judgement of the nations and the judgement of believers. The Church has already been judged at the judgement seat of Christ. Now it is time for Christ Jesus to pronounce verdict upon all others. These nations are comprised of only two groups – Israel and Gentile nations. Israel will be judged separately from the other nations. The Gentile nations are the remnant of people remaining on the Earth who were not part of Israel. They will be judged immediately before, during, and after the millennium. Judgement for them begins at the battle of Armageddon. This is the concluding judgement of people before the millennium begins.

Gentile Nations

Christ's Seat of Judgement for the Nations

There are approximately 75 days, which elapse after the overthrow of the Antichrist during Armageddon. He causes havoc upon the Earth for 1260 days. However, the book of Daniel records a final number of 1335 days. This gives us a difference of 75 days (Dan. 12:12). Some have assumed that during this period of time the judgement of the nations is taking place. During the 75 days, all preliminaries to the millennial kingdom are completed. This time period must include the judgement of the nations following the tribulation and the battle of Armageddon. It is in Matthew chapter 25 that we pick up this.

Starting with verse 31 thru verse 46, we see an episode of a tribunal that is held for "all nations". Although Christ is seated on a throne, it is not the judgement seat for believers. The preceding parable addressed the judgement of Christ's **servants** (Matt. 25:14-30). The people here differ in that they are not concluded to be servants but "nations". These nations consist of all the people who lived throughout the tribulation and were not participants in the battle of Armageddon.

At this event, both the good angels and the overcoming saints help Christ Jesus in facilitating judgement upon the nations (Matt. 25:31; 1 Cor. 6:2; Jude 1:14, 15). There will be other thrones present and the angels will actually be the ones gathering these nations together (Dan. 7:22; Matt. 16:27). The people of these nations are not judged as a whole. Each person is judged individually. They are simply called nations because they represent all remaining people of the Earth after the Church is removed.

These nations will be separated into two groups. One group will be positioned on the right, the sheep; the other will be on the left, the goats (Matt. 25:33). One's success or failure will be determined by how they treated Jews during the tribulation (Rev. 7:4-8, 12:6). Based upon the King's approval, those who are placed to his right will be allowed to "inherit the kingdom". Those positioned on the left will be sent to spend eternity in the lake of fire (Matt.25:41-46).

What does it mean to "inherit the kingdom?" Witness Lee says, "After the judgement at Christ's throne of glory, the 'sheep' will be transferred into the millennium to be the people living under the kingly rule of Christ and the overcoming believers (Rev. 2:26-27; 20:4-6) and under the priestly ministry of the saved Jews (Zech. 8:20-23). In this way the 'sheep' will inherit the (coming) kingdom. In the millennium there will be three sections: (1) the Earth, where the blessing of God's creation will be, as mentioned in Gen. 1:28-30; (2) the nation of Israel in Canaan, from the Nile to the Euphrates, from which the saved Jews will rule over the whole Earth (Isa. 60:10-12; Zech. 14:16-18); and (3) the heavenly and spiritual section (1 Cor. 15:50-52), the manifestation of the kingdom of heavens, where the overcoming believers will enjoy the kingdom reward (Matt. 5:20, 7:21). The kingdom that the 'sheep' will inherit consists of the first section."[1] To inherit the kingdom is a special privilege that some individuals out of the nations will be allowed to have (Prov. 10:30). Although Christ allows them access into his kingdom, there is no mention of them reigning.

The Battle of Armageddon

During the tribulation, there will be those who are saved (Dan. 12:12; Rev. 7:13-15). However, others will be seduced by the Antichrist during the tribulation through a great deception of miracles, lies and blasphemies (2 Thes. 2:8-12; Rev. 13:3-5). Humankind will begin to believe that the Antichrist is the most powerful person in the entire world. They will begin to question, *"Who is like the beast, and who is able to wage war with him"* (Rev. 13:4)? By the end of the tribulation (3 ½ yrs. or 42 months), he has gained absolute control over the entire Earth (Dan. 7:25).

All the people alive during the tribulation know that the Church has been raptured but they see no intervention from God. Indeed, the Antichrist continues to show his dominance by blaspheming God and by making "war with the saints" and overcoming them (Rev. 13:7). Continuing his show of power, many people will begin to believe that he can defeat even God.

The Antichrist will marshal nations into a great battle called Armageddon. This battle will last for one day and those who fight against Christ will physically be put to death with the blood trail extending for approximately 185-200 miles long and about the height of a horses bridle (Joel 3:9-17; Rev. 14:19, 20, 16:14-21, 19:15, 19).

Every person who follows the Antichrist into this battle will experience a vicious and brutal physical death which will be the initiation of the judgement of the nations.

Judgement During the Millennium

Those of the nations who were allowed to inherit the kingdom will continue to be judged during the 1000-year reign of Christ. Of course we know that Christ will be the supreme judge but he will not rule in the millennium by himself. He will allow those believers who were overcomers in the Church to judge the world with him (1 Cor. 6:2; Jude 1:14, 15; Rev. 2:26-27).

In more than one place in the scriptures, it is written that we have been made "kings and priests" (Rev. 5:10). The word king speaks of believers who will rule over the nations in the millennial kingdom (Matt. 25:21; Luke 19:17; 1 Cor. 6:2; Rev. 2:26, 5:10, 20:4). Our job will be to make sure every Gentile nation is subject to the rule of Christ.

Judged at Gog and Magog

This is humanity's last rebellion against God. The people of this group are different from those who will participate in the battle of Armageddon. In reference to this last uprising, there is a key phrase recorded in chapter twenty of Revelation. It states that after the 1000 years are finished, Satan will be released from his prison to deceive the nations **again,** leading them into another battle called "Gog and Magog" (Rev. 20:3, 7, 8).

At the close of the millennium, Satan, instead of the Antichrist, will seduce all the rebellious people of the nations who refused to submit to Christ into this last battle.

It is so amazing that sin is this powerful. Undoubtedly, embedded in the mind of the people of the nations is the reality of Armageddon. Marshalling people into that battle is more understandable than those will participate in Gog Magog.

Christ had not returned yet to overthrow his enemies; therefore, many concluded that Armageddon would be a place of victory for those who desired to usurp Christ's authority. However, the battle of Gog and Magog is completely different. Those who will join in this battle have visibly witnessed Christ's reign from Jerusalem for 1000 years. Yet, Satan is able to deceive people into this battle that will culminate in certain defeat.

The participants in Gog and Magog will have the same fate as those in Armageddon – death. The people in the Armageddon encounter were destroyed by the word of judgement from Christ whereas those here are killed by an exterminating fire from God (Rev. 20:9).

The Nations in Eternity

The remnant of nations who do not follow Satan into the battle of Gog and Magog will be transferred into eternity to live upon the new Earth. They will not be a part of the Church. We will live in the New Jerusalem with God and Christ (Rev. 21:2, 3).

These nations will have freedom to move about in eternity between the New Earth and the New Jerusalem, demonstrated by the fact that the gates of the New Jerusalem will remain open continuously, enabling the kings of the nations to bring their wealth and great treasures of their cities to pay homage to Christ.

Israel

Judged During the Tribulation

Israel will undergo progressive judgement like that of the Gentile nations. They will be judged during the tribulation, at Christ's second coming and during the millennium. Their judges will be Christ and the apostles.

The tribulation will begin the time of judgement and purging of Israel. One writer states that, "The Scriptures have given us many reasons why the tribulation will come. Some of these include: to feed Israel with judgement...to destroy the fat and strong of Israel; because Israel has forgotten the God of their salvation, and they have not kept in mind the rock of their strength, which is Jesus; to cause Israel to seek Jesus and be obedient to His Word... During this time, two-thirds of Israel will be cut off and die, but one-third shall be refined and brought through this horrible period."[2] The tribulation will cause Israel to recognize and accept Jesus as their Messiah (Zech. 13:8, 9; Rev. 7:3-8).

Jesus says to his disciples that a terrible time would be coming in which they would experience great trials, even death. The Lord states that if they would be faithful to him while undergoing these trials, at the end of this time they would be saved (Matt. 24:13). During this period, the continuous preaching of the Messiah's coming kingdom keeps people focused on the future (Matt. 24:14).

Chapter twelve of the book of Revelation shows how Israel will be attacked by Satan throughout the tribulation. Israel will end up fleeing into what is called a "wilderness" (Rev. 12:6). This coincides with the events described by Christ in Matthew (Matt. 24:9-22).

There will be 144, 000 Israelites who are sealed in their foreheads to be preserved in the wilderness for 1260 days, through God's provision, escaping death (Rev. 7:3-8, 12:6). Verses 13-16 of Revelation chapter twelve are a clear reminder of the events that happened to the Israelites when they were delivered from the Egyptians and nurtured in the wilderness. This shows that God will provide for them in almost the same way that He supernaturally provided for Israel after the Exodus.

Judged During the Millennium

The end result for Israel is that "all Israel will be saved" (Rom. 11:26). They would believe in the Messiah that they rejected for so long. During the millennium, Christ along with the twelve apostles will judge the twelve tribes.

The apostle Peter asked Jesus a question saying, *"Behold, we have left everything and followed You; what then will there be for us"* (Matt. 19:27)? Jesus responded by showing them what type of distinguished privileges they would have in the millennium. He responds, *"...you who have followed Me, in the regeneration when the Son of Man will sit on his glorious throne, you also shall sit upon twelve thrones, judging the twelve tribes of Israel"* (Matt. 19:28).

Christ will give the 12 apostles, as kings and rulers, the special privilege of making judicial decisions concerning Israel. Israel will live by their rules. If these laws are violated, they also will have power to determine what punishment is necessary.

The Judgement of the Antichrist

Daniel chapter 11 mentions a king who takes a particular disposition against God. Although the text probably refers to the Seleucid king Antiochus Epiphanes (He ruled the Jews from 175-164 BCE), many believe that he is the symbol of the Antichrist (Dan. 11:36).

As this man of sin comes into prominence, he will begin to exalt himself above every known god. The Antichrist will even speak against God himself until Christ returns for judgement (2 Thes. 2:4; Rev. 13:5, 6). In addition, during the tribulation he will be allowed to make war with the saints and to overcome them (Rev. 13:7).

At the conclusion of those years, Christ will return with his overcoming saints and wage war against the Antichrist and his armies (Jude 1:14, 15; Enoch chapter II). Those who follow the Antichrist are killed while he and the false prophet are cast alive into the lake of fire being the first to experience its torments (Rev. 19:20).

The Great White Throne Judgement

The great white throne is the concluding judgement for people groups and eternal beings (Rev. 20:11-15). This includes all the people from the millennium, unbelievers, the fallen angels and demons.

The title that John gives to this judgement seat is worthy of notation. It is "great" in comparison to all other thrones (Dan. 7:9). This speaks of its stature and height. This throne is exalted above any other throne.

The color "white" represents the majesty and purity of this judgement. The final judgement is just and right. The judge is righteous enough to send every unbeliever and rebellious angel to the lake of fire.

The person seated upon this throne is none other than Christ Jesus. He is pictured as one who is so enraged that "Earth and heaven" fled. It is time for him to administer judgement to all of his enemies. Now begins the actual resurrection process of the unrighteous (John 5:28, 29).

The seas release their captives as well as the personalities of death and Hell (Rev. 20:13). After everyone is assembled, we are made aware of the presence of books. There are "books" that are opened as well as "the book of life." These two categories of books serve two different purposes.

The "book of life" is opened to show that there are individuals at this throne of judgement who are saints. These individuals lived during the millennium but for some reason died. God raises them now to undergo judgement.

The "books" represent the record of every person's deeds (Rev. 20:12). Everything that a person does in life is noted by God. When the time of judgement arrives, every person's activities are brought before God.

After the judgement is completed, there is the introduction of the lake of fire. As the enemies of God, death, Hell and every unbeliever are thrown into this lake.

The Lake of Fire

Some theologians believe this lake is merely symbolic of the torments to be experienced by every person sent there while other theologians believe it is a literal place (Ps. 140:10). It is my belief that this is a literal place. Whatever you presume about the lake of fire, one thing is for sure, it will be a place of extreme anguish and torment.

I would like to point out a few characteristics of this Hell fire. First, just as believers will be allowed to experience more of the joyous fellowship with the Lord than others, similarly, some unbelievers will experience more torment of this lake of fire than others (Matt. 11:21-24 25:20-30; Luke 10:12-15).

In Matthew, Jesus is instructing the twelve disciples about sending them out to minister (Matt. 10:5). He makes a statement to them about those who would not believe their words. He states, *"Truly I say to you, it will be more tolerable for the land of Sodom and Gomorrah in the day of judgement than for that city"* (Matt. 10:15).

The words "more tolerable" hold great significance. These are words of comparison and indicate a varying degree of punishment according to opportunities given and the sins committed.

In other words, Sodom and Gomorrah will have it easier when it comes down to them being punished than for those who had the gospel message preached to them and rejected it. The same statement is made concerning those who experienced Jesus' mighty works (Matt. 11:20-24).

Next, we see that this fire is eternal. This word directly opposes the teaching of annihilation. Instruction concerning annihilation states that when you physically die, you cease to exist. Why would there need to be an unquenchable fire if there was the termination of life when you die physically?

The book of Revelation unambiguously asserts that this lake of fire will have the presence of brimstone and they will be *"tormented day and night forever and ever"* (Rev. 20:10). These two elements show that this fire will burn perpetually along with those who are in it.

Along with this, the gospel of Mark shows the preserving element of salt (Mark 9:49). The most common view of this is that salt is used to preserve the sinners in Hell fire. This is further indication that God intends for people to spend eternity in this fire.

Another element of this lake of fire is the mention of worms that will not die (Mark 9:44, 46, 48). This statement is obviously borrowed from Isaiah. The prophet states, *"...for their worm will not die..."* (Isa. 66:24). This is a very vivid picture of the torment of this future judgement. The presence of undying worms indicates that there must be undying bodies of people to feed on. The worms feeding on flesh is indicative of unending suffering.

Finally, this lake of fire is referred to as the "second death" (Rev. 20:14). There are only two deaths that can be experienced. The first is physical death, or separation of the soul and spirit from the body. This first aspect of death has been appointed all humankind; however, there are some who will not meet this appointment (Heb. 9:27).

The second death is a point of separation but not like the first. In the second death, unbelievers are eternally separated from any relations with God. It will be a time of immense agony. People will be confronted with regret as they think about the opportunities they missed (Matt. 13:42).

The Judgement of the Earth

Even the Earth has to be redeemed from the curse that is upon it (Gen. 3:17; Isa. 24:6). It has been continuously affected by the judgements that God brought upon Satan and humankind. It was first thrown into catastrophic disarray when Satan was judged by God, being cast to the Earth (Isa. 14:12; Jer. 4:23-26; Luke 10:18). Therefore, God had to **recreate** the Earth, which was accomplished in six days (Gen. 1:2). The emphasis in Genesis is that the Earth "became empty and chaotic" because something happened.

Some 2300 years (give or take) after the Earth was created, it experienced another aspect of judgement upon it. The Earth was flooded. Every person and animal that was not in Noah's ark was killed. The Earth suffered massive devastation.

The Earth will undergo severe devastation during the

last days, concluding with its judgement by fire. The land will suffer severe devastation, the Earth will be ravaged by a mix of hail and fire so that a third part of the Earth is burnt up and one-third of the seas will be corrupted (Rev. 6:5, 6, 7:3, 8:7-9).

This Earth will experience God's final act of judgement upon it by fire (2 Pet. 3:10-12). Notice, the judgement seat of Christ will be a trial by fire (1 Cor. 3:13), the final judgement of unbelievers will conclude with an experience of fire (Rev. 20:14, 15) and the Earth will be done away with by fire (2 Pet. 3:10-12). This is God's truest way of examining, purging and sentencing.

Now after all the devastation has taken place, God will change the Earth into the state that it should have always been. This "New Earth" will become a distinct work of art that no painter could fathom (Ps. 102:25-27).

The word "new" speaks of superiority. Both the new heaven and Earth will be vastly superior to even the best experience that we can have on Earth now. This has been the expectation of believers throughout the ages (Isa. 66:22, 23; 2 Pet. 3:13).

One of the key features of the new Earth is that there will be no more sea. The absence of the sea represents two things. I believe there had to be the removal of the seas in order to prepare the Earth for the mass of individuals that will inhabit it.

Another reason is stated by two individuals. The first states, "To the Jewish mind, the sea was a place of separation and evil. Already in the Book of Revelation it is shown to be the source of the Satanic beast (Rev. 13:1) and the place of the dead (Rev. 20:13)... In other passages of

Scripture, the sea is associated with the heathen (Isa. 57:20) and in a more general sense, with the opponents of the Lord that must be conquered (Ps. 89:9)."³

Another writer takes this approach a slight bit further. He writes, "The sea is a result of the waters of judgement, which God used to judge the pre-Adamic world. The work of God's recreation was to recover the land by restricting the result of the waters of judgement (Gen. 1:9-10; Jer. 5:22) [Ps. 104:6-9]. The living creatures of the pre-Adamic world, after being judged by the waters, became the sea's inhabitants, the demons. After...the sea has given them up to the judgement of the great white throne (Rev. 20:13), the sea will not be needed...Hence, *the sea is no more* indicates that Satan and his evil followers will all be dealt with and will not be found in the new heaven and new Earth."⁴ From this author's perspective, the seas became the place of judgement for demons. They are consigned to the depths of the Earth through means of water. Once they have been released, for final judgement, God no longer has any need for seas.

The nations who live on the new Earth will also have plenty of sunlight. There will be no need to worry about an ozone layer because the extreme brightness of God's glory will become the new light, and Christ will be its container (Rev. 21:23). Through this, the Shekinah of New Jerusalem will become the sun for the new Earth.

So the act of eternal judgement has been concluded. Everything is expressed according to a new order. Satan, the antichrist, rebellious angels, demons and unbelievers have been cast into the lake of fire. Free from all evil and impurity, we begin to live life in eternity.

MOVING ON TO SPIRITUAL MATURITY

The author concludes the section with the challenge – move on to spiritual maturity. The final verse of our foundational passage declares that we will move on to perfection "if God permits" (Heb. 6:3). The goal God has in mind for you is spiritual maturity.

You do not have to do anything to grow physically – just live. However, spiritual growth is a decision that does not happen automatically. Make the decision to put forth the effort to attain spiritual growth. Sure, there are sacrifices of your time and thoughts; however, the results of work will yield great dividends. Your insights about God, life and ministry will significantly change.

Now that you have examined all six principles, you must ensure that they are adequately and consistently understood and applied to your life in order for you to move on to spiritual maturity.

Have you been saved six months, one year, five years or even 20 and still fail to comprehend these basic truths? It is time for you to progress from the elementary teachings into the deep things. However, it is impossible to understand the deep things of God without first comprehending these ABC's of Christ.

A great problem exists among the saints. It seems like we grow in knowledge about so many things except God. Many believers find themselves in the same spiritual condition month after month and year after year. At some point in time, you should be growing into spiritual adulthood, feeding others with the true knowledge of Christ instead of others having to feed you again.

If these beginning principles are not thoroughly understood and applied, God does not give permission for his sons or daughter to go on to maturity. The writer to the Hebrews considers spiritual maturity as being able to understand higher truths.

The Bible says that God must give you a permit to continue building upon your foundation of knowledge and experience. The word "permit" means to give one a license or to allow. This does not mean that God is unwilling or has to give an okay somehow for you to advance. If you are diligent in studying the Word of God, you will advance in your knowledge concerning Him.

This statement speaks of reliance upon God's aide. In essence, the writer was saying "if God helps us" we would grow. That is, your effort alone is not enough. It takes God working with you and in you by His Spirit enabling you to understand these truths.

You learning of these "first principles" gives way to spiritual growth. Your future construction of spiritual life and ministry are contingent upon your present preparation in these basic truths. The bottom line is this. If you do not lay a proper foundation, you will make it difficult to attain proper spiritual growth.

If fulfilling God's will is the goal of your life, and if you need to grow to fulfill His will, then these questions must be asked. How can we grow properly if we do not lay a proper foundation? If you fail to grow properly, how can you ever hope to arrive at God's conclusion for your life? If you fail to arrive at your God-given destiny, how can you ever hope to be pleasing to God?

Let's move forward. Become a person of spiritual depth. It is my prayer that as each of you study this material; you will begin or continue the process of growing into a "full-grown man" being equipped for every "good work".

Index

Endnotes

The Doctrine of Baptisms

[1] Joseph Thayer's Greek-English Lexicon of the New Testament

[2] I am indebted to James Lee Beall for the points of A-C that I extracted from his book Laying The Foundation. The other points I borrowed from an article written by Wayne Jackson entitled Why Was Jesus Baptized?

[3] Wikipedia, Baptism for the Dead, http://www.en.wikipedia.org/wiki/Baptism_for_the_dead.

[4] Tony Warren, What Does It Mean To Be Baptized For The Dead?, http://www.mountainretreatorg.net/faq/baptizedforthedead.html.

[5] What does The Bible Mean When It Refers To The Baptism Of The Dead?, http://www.christiananswers.net/q-eden/edn-r001.html.

[6] Unknown author, Baptism For The Dead.

The Resurrection of the Dead

[1] The Resurrection of Jesus, http://www.aboutbibleprophecy.com/loj7htm.

[2] Joseph H. Thayer, Thayer's Greek-English Lexicon of the New Testament, #5001, p. 613.

Eternal Judgement

[1] Witness Lee, The New Testament Recovery Version, Matt. 25:34 note #1, p.145.

[2] Http://www.zhinanpost.com/Documents/Doctrines/Judgement_of_Israel_part1.htm, Judgement Of Israel During the Tribulation Part - 1.

[3] David Guzik, Revelation 21 - A New Heavens, A New Earth, And A New Jerusalem, www.enduringword.com/commentaries/6621.htm.

[4] Witness Lee, The New Testament Recovery Version, Revelation 21:1 p. 1323.

QUICK ORDER FORM

Fax Orders to: 253-520-6804

Email Orders: deepertruthspublishing@yahoo.com

Postal Orders: Deeper Truths Publishing, P.O. Box 6611, Kent WA 98031-9998

Please send the following books. I understand that I may return any of them for a full refund – for any reason, no questions asked. Cost **$16.95** (U.S. currency) + shipping **$3.00** in U.S. only.

_____

_____

_____

Please send more FREE information on:

☐ Other books

☐ Speaking/Seminars

☐ Newsletter

Name: _____

Address: _____

City: _____State: _____ Zip: _____

Telephone: _____

Email address: _____

QUICK ORDER FORM

Fax Orders to: 253-520-6804

Email Orders: deepertruthspublishing@yahoo.com

Postal Orders: Deeper Truths Publishing, P.O. Box 6611, Kent WA 98031-9998

Please send the following books. I understand that I may return any of them for a full refund – for any reason, no questions asked. Cost **$16.95** (U.S. currency) + shipping **$3.00** in U.S. only.

_____

_____

_____

Please send more FREE information on:

☐ Other books

☐ Speaking/Seminars

☐ Newsletter

Name: _____

Address: _____

City: _____State: _____ Zip: _____

Telephone: _____

Email address: _____

QUICK ORDER FORM

Fax Orders to: 253-520-6804

Email Orders: deepertruthspublishing@yahoo.com

Postal Orders: Deeper Truths Publishing, P.O. Box 6611, Kent WA 98031-9998

Please send the following books. I understand that I may return any of them for a full refund – for any reason, no questions asked. Cost **$16.95** (U.S. currency) + shipping **$3.00** in U.S. only.

_____

_____

_____

Please send more FREE information on:

- ☐ Other books
- ☐ Speaking/Seminars
- ☐ Newsletter

Name: _____

Address: _____

City: _____ State: _____ Zip: _____

Telephone: _____

Email address: _____

www.ingramcontent.com/pod-product-compliance
Lightning Source LLC
LaVergne TN
LVHW051625080426
835511LV00016B/2173